SERVE TO LEAD:

True Lessons about Lean Organizational Leadership

The Manual to Servant Leadership Principles, Agile Project Management, Start-Up Kanban, and Why Leaders Eat Last

© Copyright 2019 - All rights reserved.

from various sources. Please consult a licensed professional before attempting any techniques outlined in this book.

By reading this document, the reader agrees that under no circumstances is the author responsible for any losses, direct or indirect, which are incurred as a result of the use of information contained within this document, including, but not limited to, — errors, omissions, or inaccuracies.

Your Free Gift

As a way of saying thanks for your purchase, we're offering a free companion gift that's exclusive to readers of *Serve to Lead*.

With the companion gift, you'll discover a collection of updated recipes, checklists and useful bonus information that we couldn't fit into this book. Get the most out of this book, by getting the free companion here:

>> Go Here to Get The Free Serve to Lead Book Companion <<

https://www.book-companion.com/servant-leadership-book-companion

Would you like to listen to the Serve to Lead in your car? Get the **free Audible version** of this book on Audible.com. More information on the free promotion can be found on the companion website linked above.

Table of Contents

Introduction

Congratulations on downloading your personal copy of *Serve to Lead - True Lessons about Lean Organizational Leadership: The Manual to Servant Leadership Principles, Agile Project Management, Start-Up Kanban, and Why Leaders Eat Last.* Thank you for doing so. Chances are you have chosen to download this book because you are currently in a leadership position, and you are hoping to find a way to become a better, stronger leader. Perhaps you feel that the people you are leading don't respect you or maybe you feel like you are not motivating your team effectively. It is also possible you are not currently in a leadership role, but you are hoping to be promoted into one.

Regardless of your current position and experience as a leader, you have chosen a book that has all the tools you need to become the best leader possible. This book is going to take you by the hand and show you exactly what a good leader is and how you can become someone who is strong and sure of themselves and their leadership role. No matter how great of a leader you are today, you will see that, after reading this book, you can be an even better one without having to devote a lot of money and time into expensive programs.

Written out in clear, easy-to-read chapters, this book is going to provide you with practical outlines and tips about all of the qualities a good leader possesses. We all know that sometimes just knowing the information isn't enough, so you are also going to be given some questions you can ask yourself. These questions are going to help you understand the traits we are talking about and learn how to put the traits into practice.

Chapter 1:
Origins of Servant Leadership

When you walk into the office of Amiable Homes Real Estate Company, your attention is immediately drawn to an eye-catching poster with a slogan that says, "Happy Employees Equal Happy Customers." For the employees at Amiable Homes, those words are more than just a slogan used to welcome clients. They describe just how employees are handled and treated around here.

They are the motto the general manager, James, uses when leading his team. He views the employees as the company's greatest asset, so as a leader, he always puts their needs first. When you look around the office, you can see that his leadership style works. Enthusiasm and satisfaction are clear with every one of James's team members.

So what is James's secret?

It is simple; James employs the philosophy of servant leadership in his managerial duties. Under that philosophy, managers give attention and priority to their employees as well as to the company or organization at large. His goal in leadership is to help employees who are doing badly to do well and those that are doing well to do even better.

At Amiable Homes, each employee under James knows that he is there for them. He often checks in with them to find out how they are doing at work. He also helps them develop the necessary skills to advance their careers.

James makes decisions with the team's best interest in mind. He strives to view situations from the perspective of other staff members. He has created a conducive environment with sufficient knowledge and resources that his employees need to meet their targets. As a result, the team has been successful in meeting target goals, and staff turnover has decreased. James is an example of why servant leadership works. He is proof that servant leadership is the ideal leadership style. Before we can dive headfirst into the information that is going to make you a better servant leader, we must first look at exactly what leadership is. It will be hard to be a successful leader if you don't fully understand what it is you are trying to be successful at.

This isn't referring to just the things you need to carry out as a leader. This extends to how you should treat your team, as well as how to best motivate and encourage them to succeed. As a leader, the success of your team is a direct measurement of how well you are able to lead. If your team is often seen as being unsuccessful, then you should reevaluate how you function as a leader before you begin firing your team and hiring new people. Ask yourself if you have all of the important traits a leader should possess.

Leadership

Many people consider leadership to be a simple, easily defined word, and when asked to define a leader, they can quickly and easily explain what leadership may mean to them. In reality, leadership means different things to different people, and this increases the complexity of the definition.

There are many facets to leadership, and people tend to define the word by which facets of the role are most important to them. To be an effective leader, then, it is important that you are able to succeed at all facets of leadership. This enables anyone who is viewing you in your leadership role to view you as a strong leader, and it also allows you to be a good leader to all types of team members and not just certain types of people.

For instance, an individual in a management position may define leadership as the ability to lead a team to produce effective results since it is the results that someone in this position is focused on. However, someone who is on the team may define leadership as the ability to understand the skills each team member brings to the table and to assign the jobs according to those skills. Since the second person is on the team, the leader's people skills are more important to him than they are to the manager. Both of these definitions are correct, but neither is complete.

To keep the definition simple and short, we are going to define leadership as someone who brings together the skills to:

- Create an inspiring vision of what the future holds;

- Motivate and inspire people to want to engage with the vision created;

- Manage the delivery of that vision;

- Build and coach a team that is effective at achieving the vision ("What is Leadership," 2019).

The words, "leader" and "leadership" are often misused to describe someone who is managing a team. You will realize that managers are different from leaders. Lots of individuals confuse the two—management and leadership—and that causes people to have differing opinions about how leadership is defined.

What are the Differences Between a Manager and a Leader?

The biggest difference between a manager and a leader is that a manager has people who work for them while a leader has people who follow them. For example, people who are working for a manager come into work and do their job without caring too much about the final product. On the contrary, someone who is following a leader is coming in to do his part to see the success of the final product.

This doesn't mean that a manager cannot also be a leader; in fact, to be successful you need to be both a good leader and a good manager. By effectively functioning as a manager and a leader, you are encouraging the people who work for you to be more invested in both their portion of the project and the final outcome.

Leadership is having the ability to get people to not just understand but to also believe in your vision and wanting to work with you in achieving your goals. On the other hand, managing is more about monitoring and ensuring the day-to-day tasks are happening as they should be.

Consider the following questions:

- *Do you think you are good at making sure the day-to-day tasks are being completed?*

- *Do you think you inspire the people around you to want to achieve the goals that are set out for them?*

- *Do you think you are an effective coach to the people you work with?*

- *Would you define yourself as a leader or a manager?*

- *Would your team/employees classify you as a manager or a leader?*

- *Are you ready* to do whatever it takes to become a better leader?

Leadership Styles

Do you know your leadership style? Did you even know there were different styles of leadership?

To truly understand the essence of servant leadership, you must understand the different types of leadership. You, as the leader, must evaluate yourself to recognize what kind of leadership style you naturally exhibit. This will help you choose more effectively on how to lead the team.

Individuals can sense when a leader is disingenuous about themself. Be genuine and consistent in leading the team. Acting on an unnatural style will leave an impression of uncertainty and causes your team to question your credibility to lead.

Each leadership style is unique and, based upon the presenting situation, you will leverage one style over another. The foundation of leadership will guide you on the best style to use. There is no magic combination for success. Each situation needs to be analyzed for the best approach.

In the 1930s, Kurt Lewin defined three psychology-based leadership styles: autocratic, democratic, and laissez-faire (Cherry, 2019). These styles are still commonly used today when describing leadership styles.

The autocratic style demands immediate compliance. As the word denotes, this is the do-as-you-are-told kind of leader. This kind of leadership style works best in situations that warrant immediate action. However, when used continuously, the autocratic style will result in discontent among the team. This style is effective to get people from a burning building or out of gunfire. It is effective during a code or in the critical care unit when someone goes into cardiac arrest. It is not beneficial when modifying the behavior of your team, and is often met with resistance. Be cautious when using it.

The democratic style is consensus through participation. The democratic leader is one who builds trust and achieves goals through voting, consensus, or collaboration. This kind of leader tends to ask questions and reaches agreements through two-way communication. Consider this style when you are rolling out a new process or initiative. Develop a small focus group to define the process, expectations, workflow, etc. There will always be elements you do not consider because you are not doing the job every day. Bring in your subject matter experts (i.e., team members) and collaborate. This will also provide an avenue for the team's buy-in.

The laissez-faire style is based on the mindset of building a strong team and then staying out of their way. It is the opposite of autocratic leadership. Here the individuals are given loosely defined objectives and goals. One of the most vital benefits of this style is innovation. This style can be frustrating for individuals who want clearly defined objectives.

Other researchers have identified leadership styles different from Lewin's.

In 1964, business-minded professionals Robert Blake and Jane Mouton focused on two leadership styles: task-oriented and people-oriented ("Leadership Styles–Choosing the Right Approach for the Situation," 2018).

The task-oriented style is focused on results-driven outcomes. In this style, the leader ensures clear communication and expectations of the objectives and desired outcomes. Which team member is most appropriate for the task is not considered.

The people-oriented style is focused on determining which team member is most suited for a task based upon his current skill set, interests, or personal development. This style is effective for developing an individual through stretch opportunities. Stretch opportunities are tasks given to individuals that are above his skill set and intended to push the individual out of his comfort zone to promote development.

In 2002, Daniel Goleman detailed six emotional styles of leadership: visionary, coaching, affiliate, democratic, pacesetting, and commanding (Casali, 2015).

The visionary style moves people toward a vision. This leadership style is at the top of the list in terms of being impactful. This kind of leader gains strength through passion and vision, which empowers the followers, motivating and inspiring them. It often drives innovation and creativity.

Simply put, the leader conveys the vision and gets out of the team's way.

The coaching style develops people for the future. This is a kind of leader whose focus is on achieving progress. Every single person on the team needs coaching in some capacity. For example, an individual's goal may not be a management path. Focusing on the individual's goal could be as simple as demonstrating excellence in his everyday job or enhancing his knowledge of treating diabetes.

The affiliate style creates emotional bonds. This is the people-come-first kind of leader in the sense that he tries to build a bond or relationship as much as possible. It is most effective in the motivation phase when there's a lack of inspiration among the team. This style is important to leverage when speaking with senior leaders. The team has chosen you to represent them. Keep this in mind and consider carefully how new initiatives will impact the team.

The pacesetter style expects excellence and self-direction. This is the kind of leader who is prone to set high standards without considering others' ideas. When used, it may damage team morale and make members feel inferior.

The democratic style has previously been discussed and again focuses on consensus through participation.

The commanding style is equivalent to the do-as-you-are-told autocratic style of leadership.

There are also four additional styles of leadership that are defined, and they are the main focus of leadership today.

Transactional leadership focuses on the operations that happen on a daily basis. This leader has challenges with seeing the big picture or conveying a vision. Transactional leaders keenly focus on an individual's roles and responsibilities. They aggressively manage the performance of team members who are not meeting expectations, thus leading to low morale.

Transformational leadership provides room for innovation in any firm since the aim is to keep the team inspired and motivated. These leaders are focused on transforming their organizations to the next level by leading high-performing and engaging teams. This leadership is achieved through clear communication, conveying vision, integrity, emotional intelligence, authenticity, and self-awareness. This is the most common style in business.

Charismatic leadership encompasses pertinent elements of the transformational leadership style by ensuring that there is more inspiring and motivational energy. However, this is all for the benefit of the leader. This leader is not focused on innovation or excelling in the organization. This style often leads to the demise of the organization.

Servant leadership was first defined in 1970 by Robert Greenleaf as the natural desire to lead by serving others—meeting the needs of the team members, entitling them to make decisions, focusing on growth, and ensuring their basic needs are met. A benefit of servant leadership is higher engagement, which leads to the high performance of the team. The team members feel valued and have a greater sense of engagement. They feel the leader cares about them and their well-being. The team demonstrates high morale through guidance by a moral compass. This leader leads with high integrity, focuses on the good of the organization as well as the team members, is concerned with stakeholders, and exhibits a high degree of self-awareness. There are the fundamental competencies of servant leadership that transcend all styles of leadership. Throughout the remainder of this book, you will learn these principles and when to apply them.

To be effective in leadership, one must know which style to leverage. Understanding that each style is critical depending on the situation and the environment you lead is vital to success. In general terms, leadership becomes a difficult subject to define because there isn't just one clear cut example of what leaders do and how they interact with their teams. The type of leader you are depends mainly on your personality, but regardless of which of the following four categories of leadership styles you fall into, the advice in the next chapters is going to be able to help you unleash your full potential.

1. <u>Thought Leaders</u>: These leaders use the power of their ideas to actualize change. They are able to encourage their followers by helping them to envision new possibilities and concepts in a clear way. This makes their followers want to be a part of the change that the leader is promoting.

2. <u>Courageous Leaders</u>: These leaders are ones who bravely pursue a vision, even though there are many risks and potential opposition. They are able to use their strong convictions to encourage their followers, even if the idea they are trying to promote isn't very popular among most people.

3. <u>Inspirational Leaders</u>: These leaders are leaders who are able to promote change by displaying their strong commitment to the goal they are trying to achieve. They have

incredibly positive attitudes which help them to create a strong emotional bond with their followers.

4. <u>Servant Leaders</u>: These leaders care deeply about their followers. They create a sustainable environment for the success of their followers. Since the leaders are willing to provide for their followers, the followers are encouraged and want to go an extra step to help the leaders in return.

Consider the following questions:

- *Which leadership style among the ones stated above do you feel most describes how you lead?*

- *Which styles correlate with the kind of leader you would like to be?*

- *How would you rank the leadership styles in order of most effective to least effective? Do you feel that the leadership styles can be ranked or are they all important in their own way?*

You should be able to see that you fall into more than one of the categories above and, in fact, you can likely see yourself in all four of the categories. By the time you are done going through the exercises in this book, you will have a good understanding of why all four of the styles are important and how you demonstrate related aspects in your leadership role. For now, what is most important to remember is that successful leaders come in all shapes and sizes. Regardless of what you may think of yourself and your abilities to lead successfully, you have the power to become a strong leader that people want to follow.

No two people are the same—not even twins. We are each unique human beings, and every person has physical, emotional, and mental traits unlike anyone else. The scientific reason behind this is to ensure variety in the human race, helping the species propagate (grow and spread). Imagine if all humans looked and thought alike, with the same exact interests. Everyone would strive for the same goal, the same position in the group. A group is like any machine and needs all the different parts to work properly as a whole. You can't have a group made up entirely of leaders or with all followers doing the same task. Each unique person plays an important and different role to keep a group working well. Thus, variety is a very good, healthy thing.

Personality Types and Leadership Styles

Everyone interacts with people in different ways, based on their unique personality and style. Psychologists group different types of personalities into categories, although these categories/groupings vary from one school of thought to another. Each school of thought focuses on/looks at different facets of the personality. These facets include consciousness, attitude, psychology, etc.

Carl Jung's model for personality typing is the one most used today. When we focus on attitude, Jung identifies people as being one of two types: extroverted or introverted. Extroverts acquire energy from interacting with people and socializing. Introverts gain energy from being alone. Their energy gets used up quickly during social interactions, requiring them to need more alone time to reboot and re-energize.

It is helpful for a leader to know which personality type he has as this can affect how he leads. An extrovert tends to be more widely liked than an introvert since they are more naturally suited to social situations. These people make great motivators and leaders, attracting a large, avid group of followers. That's not to say an introverted person cannot be a good leader. Though not always as popular, introverts tend to be smarter leaders who make better decisions. Introverts are some of the brightest, most successful people in the world because they take the time on their own without other people distracting them to think carefully through each decision before acting on it.

Don't let this information influence you either way. Your personality type doesn't ultimately affect your ability to be a strong leader. Many people assume that being introverted means you're shy, but that is not necessarily true. You may need to gain energy from being alone, but then you can use that energy to be vibrant and social in public. It's just that the introverts may need more time out of the public eye to be that energized social person. In any case, whether you're an extrovert or an introvert, you have the potential to be a strong, motivating leader.

We have talked about the different personality types and how those relate to leadership. Now let's take a look at different leadership styles that tend to go along with each personality type.

Authoritarian/Autocratic Leader

As the name implies, these leaders have total authority over how their group of followers acts and operates in the organization. Strict regulations, policies, or laws are enforced so that it is clear to the group what should be done or avoided in order to obey. Authoritarian leaders also tend to have a strictly professional or business relationship with their group, creating a distinct and absolute line between leader and follower. They don't want to be perceived as a "friend" or an equal; they are simply a ruler to follow without question.

Authoritarians will have managers and supervisors under them to maintain a successful rule. These managers keep a close eye on the group, overseeing the completion of necessary work and adhering to rules. Authoritarian leaders feel that this is the only way to get work done and keep order. Examples of countries ruled by this style of leadership are Cuba and North Korea. While this style can benefit those who work best under constant supervision, this type of environment becomes confining for creative people or anyone who wants to do things unconventionally.

Democratic Leader

Unlike authoritarians, this style of leader doesn't rely solely on his own decision-making abilities but depends on help from the group. Democratic leaders will debate with their followers, as well as discuss new ideas to encourage more involvement. Even though democratic leaders

27

prefer group input, it isn't a "free-for-all" style. It's group-oriented but not chaotic. The leader still sets certain guidelines that the group must adhere to.

Some people may not fully understand this kind of leader, thinking he's foolish to share any of his power with the group. However, research shows that the democratic style of leadership is often the most effective and productive.

Leader as Equal

In this style of leadership, the leader tends to shy away from supervising the group. He may believe that everyone will be happier and more productive if they are left to their own tasks. Decisions are made as a group as if everyone is equal. This style of leadership usually applies to leaders who work with people just as experienced as themselves and don't require as much supervision. If this type of leadership is applied to groups with less experience and motivation, then it could result in non-cohesiveness, lack of productivity, and general dissatisfaction.

Reward-Based Leader

This type of leader motivates the group of followers by using a reward and/or punishment system to boost the quality of work. Rewards can be tangible or psychological and given based on a good performance or a good show of effort. A tangible reward could be something monetary like a bonus or a raise. A psychological reward could be something like an employee of the month or a name in the hall of fame. If anybody doesn't meet the expectations, they are given corrective measures to improve performance. This type of leader is great for an organization that is trying to mature and be more productive in order to reach its goals.

Leader by Influence

These leaders attempt to influence the outlook of the group by finding ways to inspire them with a sense of purpose. This type of leader doesn't care how they're viewed by the group. They simply have passionate ambitions and a vision, and they strongly persist in sharing this with the group. However, they don't think of the group as sheep that will follow them blindly. Instead, they want to challenge everyone to think deeply and independently. It's not hard for a member of the group to be able to meet directly with the leader because the leader remains highly available and visible in the organization.

Every leader falls into one of these five types of leadership styles. Some may appear more effective and kinder than others, but every type has its pros and cons. None of them are perfect, but they can all operate effectively in some situations.

Chapter 2:
Building a Leadership Skill Set

You can't be an effective leader if you don't understand the skills a leader should possess. Chances are you already possess varying degrees of each of the skills listed below, and you are going to be stronger in some skills than in others (Hasan, 2017). What is important, though, is finding a balance among all of the skills. This chapter will explain some vital qualities a good leader should possess as well as some tips and tricks on how you can improve the skills you already have (Tracy, 2018).

<u>Honesty</u>: Most of us were taught to be honest, and that needs to carry over to a leader. Leaders are ethical and believe that honesty is the foundation of success. Leaders who demonstrate honesty share information openly with their team and avoid putting a false spin on things. Their team always knows where they stand with the leader, and since the leader is always honest with the team, the team is always honest with their leader.

Empathy: The best leaders praise their team in public and address problems with them in private. Good leaders are willing to guide their teams through challenges and are always on the lookout for better solutions that will foster the long-term success of the team. Good leaders focus on moving forward and looking for constructive solutions rather than looking for someone to assign blame to. Leaders who display empathy for their team members are more likely to have team members who have the willingness to go the extra mile for their leader.

Optimism: Great leaders should reflect positive energy to their teams. Leaders with optimism are courageous, and their teams trust them to offer solutions. They avoid thinking in pessimistic ways or offering too much personal criticism. Such leaders work to gain consensus from the team members. Since these leaders are always looking on the bright side, their team members are more confident with their work because they know that their leader will find a solution to any problem.

Accountability: Leaders should be willing to take responsibility for every action that happens. If challenges arise, leaders are quick to identify them and find solutions. This allows the members of a team to feel assured that their leader is going to help them be successful and not give them work that is outside of their capabilities without proper direction.

<u>Confidence</u>: People are naturally attracted to confident leaders. When challenged, a confident leader doesn't give in easily since they understand that they have invested a lot in their opinions, strategies, and ideas. They accept responsibility when proven wrong and tend to improve quickly.

<u>Decisiveness</u>: Leaders are required to make tough choices. They must understand that in certain situations, difficult decisions that reflect the best interests of the organization must be made in a timely manner. Decisive leaders know that decisions often need to be authoritative and final. At the same time, they know when to foster collaborative decision-making. Those who are following decisive leaders can trust that in the face of adversity, their leader will direct them toward success. They also know that this leader will listen to what the team has to say. A decisive leader instills confidence in the team.

<u>Awareness</u>: A good leader is aware of the team members around them. They are leaders who understand and accept the difference that exists between the boss and the workers/employees. This allows their followers to know who is leading them and trust that their leader is always going to

take them in the proper direction to attain the desired outcomes.

<u>Focus</u>: Great leaders can plan ahead and stay organized. They come up with a strategy that is tangible, monitored, and easily defined. They clearly communicate their plans. This allows those who are following to know that their leader is someone who will ensure that they reach their destination regardless of what roadblocks come up along the way.

<u>Inspiration</u>: When you combine all of the above traits, you are left with a truly inspiring leader. A true leader is someone who can communicate clearly and concisely while motivating everyone every day. They challenge their team by setting high but attainable expectations while also providing all of the support and tools that are necessary for their team to achieve those goals.

Consider such questions like:

- *Which three traits do you think best describe who you are as a leader?*

- *Which three traits do you feel you need to work on the most?*

- *Do you agree* that all of the above traits are important in a good leader?

Consider balancing all of the above skills to be a successful leader. If you have a weakness in some traits, you will find yourself in either of the following situations:

1. You are able to build and establish good relationships with people, but you are often unsuccessful at accomplishing the things you set out to do. You often struggle to keep your team motivated to get their work done.

2. You always have a clear vision of what you want to accomplish. You know what you need to do to get your team members to use their skills to the best of their abilities. However, you often forget that your team is comprised of people who also have needs.

Now that you are aware of the traits that a good leader possesses, it is time to learn the techniques needed to improve each of those traits and help you increase the level of skill you currently have. By dedicating some time to improving each of the traits listed, you are proving to yourself that you are ready to become a better leader.

Training for the Leadership Traits

Effective communication (good listening and respect)

Good leaders possess great communication skills. Communication is a very vital skill that you can use to influence other people. It is the process of exchanging or imparting information by writing, speaking, or using other mediums, and personal ideas are conveyed through communication from one person to another. When you want to speak to other people, this means that you want to communicate something to them. Strong relationships are built by positive communication. Communication is as vital in personal life as it is in business. By becoming an excellent communicator, you have the assurance of gaining support from other people.

Good leaders are known to be good communicators (Entschev, 2018). They are able to express their needs in an authentic manner, gain support from others, and move people to action. But good communication skills are not something that you're simply born with; they are something that need to be learned through continuous practice, awareness, and refinement.

The following tips can highly assist you in becoming a great communicator:

Knowing Your Objectives

Knowing your life objectives starts by clearly defining what you want to achieve in your life. Similarly, you should always consider asking yourself some questions before actually communicating. Consider understanding whether you are only interested in passing along some information and ideas or if there is something that you want from the people you plan to communicate with. This way, you will always stay focused on the goal of your communication. This will increase the possibility of communicating successfully. Before communicating on any occasion or in any situation where you want support from other people, it is always advisable to clearly state the objective of your communication.

Always Be Clear and Concise

Good communicators are known for being brief, clear, and to the point. They always have an understanding of what they want to communicate, and they always get to the point quickly and with a lot of confidence.

It is always a great idea to stop using complex acronyms and words. Yes, it will show people how well you have mastered English, but it may also alienate your audience if they cannot understand you. Always try to avoid jargon that your audience is not familiar with.

Be a Good Listener

Just like good leaders, good communicators are known to be the best listeners. You should always avoid interrupting when communicating. Ensure that you have given the other person some space when you are speaking. Allow them to ask for clarifications or corrections if needed, give them a chance to add some valuable points to the topic which you are speaking about. Always ensure that you are open to their communication and points of view. Always make them recognize that they are understood and heard.

Pay Attention to Nonverbal Cues

Our body language, facial expressions, tone of voice, posture, and eye contact, as well as gestures, convey a lot of what we say. Always have confidence when speaking so as to ensure that your nonverbal cues are not communicating different messages to your audience. You should always portray some sense of openness. Failing to make proper eye contact might imply that you are not truthful to your audience. Crossing your arms may send the message that you are uninterested in what the other person is saying. The appropriate way to communicate with other individuals is by ensuring that you are standing or sitting up straight and making firm eye contact. You should always maintain eye contact and pay close attention to their nonverbal cues.

Manage Emotions and Stress

Being extremely stressed or highly emotional may keep you from being able to think clearly about what you want to communicate. Negative or stressful thoughts lead to poor communication, and you might not get your message across in the appropriate manner. A lot of stress and emotions actually might lead you to communicate the wrong things by saying the wrong words or sending confusing or misleading nonverbal cues, as well as misreading people. To allow yourself to effectively communicate when you are emotional, you can consider taking your time to calm down, take deep breaths, and have a moment of silence. You should try to ask yourself why you are feeling a certain way. You can also explain your feelings to another person, which will allow you to empathize with their emotions and make sure they are not misreading your nonverbal cues.

Confirm and Follow Up

It is always recommended to consider asking for feedback from the person(s) you are communicating with. When doing this, ensure that they have provided the right feedback by both considering their verbal and nonverbal cues. This will assist you in avoiding any misunderstandings. If you are communicating while seated, you can follow up on the entire communication by summarizing what was discussed and asking if the person has any questions. Details of actions that will be undertaken should always be included. The people who should be responsible for such undertakings should also be included and told how long they will have to accomplish said actions.

Work on Your Written Skills

Communication is not limited to speaking. As a leader, you may be required to communicate via writing such as email, so it is important to make sure you possess good written communication. These include written documents and emails. Your writing should always be adjusted for tone based the occasion or recipient. Remember to write in a way that your audience can understand. In written communication, proofread your work to avoid errors which can lead to miscommunication and misunderstanding.

Listening Styles

What does listening mean? According to the International Listening Association (ILA), listening is the process that involves the attention, receipt, interpretation, and response to a context communicated aurally ("Types of Listening," 2019). Listening leverages more than just one of your senses.

Verbal communication relates to more than just the spoken word. The actual speaking represents only 35 percent of the real meaning when communicating. About 55 percent happens through body language communication.

On average, you listen to 450 words per minute, despite only speaking an average of 150 words per minute. Does this mean you should be able to actually process everything you hear?

No!

On average, you only process about 13 to 25 percent of what you hear.

Take a moment and think about that!

When did you last ask someone to repeat a question? How about hear a story but be unable to recall the details? Why?

In today's world, everything, including our minds, is full of distractions. These distractions are frequently on the sidelines of your subconscious mind hidden just to the right or left, creeping back onto the center stage when least expected.

It only takes one word, sound, or smell to instantly pull you from the conversation and get you lost in your own thoughts. This is natural human behavior.

Effective leadership is naturally tied to listening. The more you can actively engage yourself and your mind in listening, the more you will understand your team, its barriers, and its processes. To better understand how to be a more active or mindful listener, you need to understand the four types of listening styles ("Listening Styles," 2019).

People-oriented listening style demonstrates a strong focus on understanding the feelings of the individual who is speaking. This style leverages empathy and emotional intelligence to appeal to the individual's emotional side in arguments. One drawback to this style is the potential for judgment impairment.

Content-oriented listening style is more focused on the content quality of what is said. The focus is more on a fact-finding mission and investigation of the individual's credibility. This style is geared toward understanding the cause of an issue. One drawback to this style is the potential to completely discount communication if perceived to be from a non-credible source.

Action-oriented listening style demonstrates more of a focus on the plan or actions of individuals. Those with this style are more concrete thinkers and focus more on getting the job done. These leaders struggle with communicating about visions and large, vague concepts. Some drawbacks to this style are the perception of a lack of empathy toward the team and the appearance of losing sight of the big picture.

Time-oriented listening style is focused on the time spent listening. These leaders are more focused on getting straight to the summary points and short answers. For example, on average, physicians interrupt a patient within 18 seconds of speaking. This is a time-oriented listener. As a result, the patients are frustrated and often may never get to explain the main reason they are seeing the physician. As a leader, you could miss valuable feedback from the team because they feel you are too busy to listen.

Can you identify with one of these styles?

The most effective listening style is a combination of two or more of these styles. Like leadership styles, listening styles can be mastered with practice. It all starts with becoming an active and mindful listener.

Mastering mindful listening is at the heart of a servant-leader. If you really listen, the individual will tell you everything you need to know to be an effective leader. In the same way, if a physician simply listens without taking over the conversation, he will be able to effectively diagnose the patient.

We all spend our time mindlessly interacting and performing activities while being distracted by our subconscious. For example, you have the radio on but cannot recall the name or artist of the last song you heard. You are driving and end up at your destination but are unable to recall making the turns.

Stop. Take a deep breath. Now let's wake up that subconscious awareness.

You can practice mindful listening through the following:

1. Prepare. Clear your subconscious mind of any thoughts. You can write down what you feel you need to recall quickly. The need to recall a thought quickly is often the driving force behind why a thought remains in your subconscious mind. Managing these thoughts can be accomplished in different ways. You could be old-school and keep a small three-by-five notebook handy. You then jot down ideas to remove them from your subconscious mind and ensure that you don't forget them. Other people prefer technology and manage their thoughts on apps such as Evernote. Regardless of what you use, the next step is to remove any physical distractions from the area, such as computers, phones, and other electronic devices.

2. Be present. Focus on the words, the tone, and the body language of the speaker. Look directly at the speaker and focus. Avoid the temptation to mentally prepare a rebuttal and prevent yourself from drifting off into your thoughts. What is the individual saying? How is he or she saying it?

3. Show that you are present. Convey to the speaker that you are actively listening. Use your nonverbal cues of nodding your head, murmuring in agreement, and smiling. Additionally, exhibit an open posture with open arms, uncrossed legs, and proper posture.

4. Remove barriers while listening. Along with removing physical distractions, you must continue to remove barriers throughout the listening process by removing mental barriers. Negative thoughts such as criticism, judgment, and prejudice, can impair your ability to actively listen to the speaker. Emotions such as jealousy, fear, denial, or apathy, can also cause impairment. Be aware of your internal emotional temperature as you listen.

5. Respond appropriately. Allow the speaker to complete communicating what he wants to say. Ask clarifying questions and paraphrase what has been said. You can also periodically recap the speaker's comments. If the speaker's comments elicit an emotional response, ask for clarification on the comment. Many times, the emotional response is due to miscommunications or misunderstandings.

Mindful listening is not achieved overnight and takes practice. It is an essential skill for leadership that also can enhance your everyday life. It provides an avenue to retain more verbal information and increase attention span, self-esteem, and thoughtful speech.

Mindful listening is the essence of a leader and an essential quality as you pause to consider your words and the impact of the words. The higher your position, the more impactful your words.

Persuasion (influence)

Persuasion is a fundamental and essential part of leadership. It is not done by ill intention or manipulation. Consider persuasion as your ability to lead people in a specific direction on your behalf, regardless of your formal authoritative position.

Effective persuasion is only possible if your leadership appeals to a diverse group of individuals. You must make rational arguments and develop reasonable solutions.

To persuade your audience, you must first know your audience. Who is your audience? We convey a different message when addressing different classes or professions. Consider the occupation.

If I am persuading a clinical professional, I will focus the conservation on a medically related approach. With a mechanic or engineer, I will relate the topic to their unique occupational tasks. Know your audience and speak their language.

What's in it for me?

The number one message to communicate to an audience is the benefit of following the initiative you are conveying. The benefit must be tangible or something they can see or touch. What does the team get? Why should they follow? Think about the initiatives from all angles. Some benefits could include the following:

- Reducing the steps in a process

- Eliminating duplicate work

- Creating an automated process to eliminate manual work

- Freeing up time for more desirable activities

- Improving safety records

- Increasing status and recognition

These are just some of the potential benefits; in reality, there are countless benefits. You must know your team members to identify the best angle of persuasion. Knowing your team begins with knowing what motivates them.

Motivation: This represents the passion behind the action. Motivation is demonstrated by the desire to raise the bar and challenge the status quo continuously. Your motivation to develop leadership is demonstrated today by reading this book. Individuals like you are viewed as having high work standards and being goal-oriented and committed to continuous professional development. Motivation is contagious. People naturally surround themselves with like-minded people. You are in good company.

To motivate your team for performance, you must understand your team and leverage each individual's engagement. Team engagement manifests itself in the team members' commitment to the organization's goals or values, the commitment to the success of the company, and the commitment to do their best every day. Each team member will have a different level of engagement, which may vary based on the current initiative.

Roughly, about 28 percent of disengaged team members leave a company, while only 4 percent are highly engaged. Many times, leaving is not financially driven. Consider the impact of having to replace an individual:

- Increased workload

- Downtime

- Training for the new staff

- Potential for fragmented care or failure to manage patients properly

- Patients stop following treatment plans

You need to create the opportunity to leverage your leadership skills to drive engagement within your team.

You need to start by meeting the team members where they are and identifying the three levels of engagement:

Highly engaged: Think superstars—individuals who think about the job outside of working hours and don't consider the job "work." These individuals generally make your job easier. They are open to change and innovation. They are always working toward the end goal and looking for opportunities for growth.

Engaged: Think solid performers—individuals who consistently provide good work. Engaged individuals are essential for every team. These are the worker bees. These individuals are happy to do their jobs and do not desire additional responsibility. They are followers of the direction you set rather than active participants in evolving the model.

Disengaged: Think individuals who are not aligned with the position, team, mission, etc.— high-maintenance individuals or underperformers. They can drag the team down. Many times, they require most of your attention and management. These individuals can distract the team from the end goal, create chaos, and increase team drama. This instills uncertainty in your team.

Where do most of your team fall? Generally, 10 percent will be highly engaged, 80 percent engaged, and 10 percent disengaged.

To leverage engagement, you must know where you currently stand with your team. Ask for their honest feedback without fear of reciprocation. It is vital to your growth as their leader. You will know where you need to adjust your shortcomings and focus on personal growth. Instill on the team the importance of providing you feedback as their leader. Reward the team for feedback. Keep in mind the importance of partnership and growing together.

Engaging the team must be done through a cultural change, not by creating a program.

Programs simply result in your superstars continuing to thrive as the unengaged continue with the status quo. A motivated individual will work hard when there is something in it for them, while an engaged one will work hard for the sake of the company.

What is the best technique to engage a group of individuals? The most effective technique I have discovered is described in Paul Marciano's *Carrots, and Sticks Don't Work*. The RESPECT model is an acronym for the most effective aspects of engagement.

RESPECT represents recognition, empowerment, supportive feedback, partnership, expectations, consideration, and trust.

Recognition: Each team member desires to do a good job and be acknowledged for his or her commitment to the team. This will reinforce to the team what the preferred behavior is. Know your individual's preferred method of recognition. Many, but not all, welcome being recognized in front of other team members; however, individuals with underlying social anxiety will shy away and be embarrassed by public recognition. This could impede their future actions on goals. By knowing each of your team members, you will know their preferred way to be recognized.

Empowerment: Install in your team the trust to make decisions and function independently. You must support them through this avenue regardless of the decision made. Be mindful of micromanagement and ensure that your team feels supported; this will help them to develop the confidence needed to make more important decisions without questioning themselves. Delegate tasks that will showcase their unique skills.

Supportive feedback: Your job is to communicate feedback to the team to facilitate growth and an understanding of the goals and initiatives. Note that this feedback is supportive. The team members must receive the information as a personal growth opportunity, not a punitive one. Everyone is unique. You must identify the appropriate tone and structure of the conversation to instill the feedback without damaging the relationship.

Partnership: Leaders are partners with our team, not bosses. You are moving toward the same goal with slightly different jobs. You push each other to excel in your role and to win as a team. You leverage transparency by ensuring the team is in the know of the current happenings. In return, they are open with you about the team's functioning.

Expectations: These are the defined goals that support the company's mission. As mentioned in the communication section, you must be clear in your expectations. The expectations should be clearly communicated and in writing to limit the confusion of the team. You must also reinforce the expectations to keep the team on task and focused on the immediate prioritization. Vague expectations lead to underperforming teams and are a poor reflection of your leadership.

Considerations: This refers to giving careful thought of how to interact with an individual. Leverage your emotional intelligence skills and understand the position of each individual as it is rooted in his or her personality. Team members will feel you care for them and feel respected. Ask for the input of the individual doing the specific process before making changes that directly impact his or her daily activities. There is a high likelihood that they will provide you valuable feedback on how to increase efficiency. Make sure they know you have their best interest in mind and are not checking up on them while they are performing the job.

Trust: Trust is a common theme here, which should impress on you the value of trust among your team within your leadership role. This is the most pivotal element of any leader. It has the ability to make a good leader great and a mediocre leader bad.

Know where you currently stand with your team and ask for their feedback. It is vital to your growth as their leader. You will know where you need to adjust your shortcomings and focus on personal growth. Instill in the team the importance to provide you feedback as their leader and stress the aspect of rewarding the team for feedback. Keep in mind the partnership and the process of growing together.

Empathy

As leaders, one of your greatest strengths is empathy. However, allowing the emotion to make business objectives personal can be your greatest weakness. Remember not to make things personal and not to carry the weight of others' problems. Recognize that upset patients, customers, clients, and senior leaders are a result of anger at the situation or outcome. It is not reflective of how they personally feel about you.

Empathy is your ability to understand someone's feelings. Developing empathy with the ability to manage your own emotions demonstrates emotional intelligence. Developing the ability to recognize and manage emotions improves your professional disposition.

Empathy is not a sign of weak leadership, nor does it denote that you will give into every concern of your team. Empathy does not replace our personality. Also, it does not indicate that you will assume the personal strife or emotional baggage of an individual.

Emotional intelligence is not a reflection of one's IQ and has nothing to do with intellect. Does this imply that you can never have a bad day as a leader? Absolutely *not*! Every leader has good days and bad days.

However, it is important to consider how your disposition will impact the team. For example, if having an off day that significantly impacts your mood and ability to interact with others, consider rescheduling a team meeting. Over time, you will develop techniques that will help you with the analysis and processing of bad days to limit interruptions of your schedule.

Empathy provides the ability to develop trust with your team. The trust will provide an avenue for the team to share concerns with you. Consider encouraging your team members to proactively provide you information about a disgruntled individual or notification if they hear your project is missing the goal. Effective leaders take the time to understand and address the individual's concerns.

Sometimes individuals just want to vent or share with you what is happening. They do not expect any action. They just want the ability to share with a trusted leader. You must recognize when you need to respond. Timing is everything. Team members sharing concerns demonstrates the comfort to show their vulnerable side. This warrants the respect of your prompt attention, or you will lose similar future opportunities.

Be mindful of how you interact with an individual. Leverage empathy and understand the position of each individual as it is rooted in his or her personality. The team will feel you care for them and feel respected.

Always be sure to talk to an individual before making adjustments to his or her job. They most likely are more familiar with the work and may be able to provide you with valuable feedback that will improve the job. Be sure to make sure your team members know that you trust them and that checking on their work does not mean you doubt their abilities.

Why is empathy important in leadership? What is in it for you as a leader?

As a leader, your empathy will create a sense of trust between you and your team members, which will strengthen your leadership of the team and lead to greater collaboration and engagement. Remember, the higher the team engagement, the higher the performance.

Some additional benefits of enhancing empathy would include:

- Ability to understand the root cause of unengaged team members or poor performers

- Ability to support struggling individuals to succeed

- Enhancement of professional relationships

- Virtual window into the team

Developing empathy begins by actively listening to an individual when they speak. Try to hear beyond what they are saying and focus on how it is said. Do you hear excitement, anger, or frustration?

Next, you must put yourself in the shoes of your team. Understand their challenges and victories. What are their pain points? View initiatives from all sides and even have a few colleagues to bounce ideas off of. Also, encourage the team members to share how they feel about situations. Ask yourself why the individual conveys _____ (fill in the emotion) when speaking.

Create and sustain relationships (no more transactional thinking) and create more leaders (no more self-serving behavior)

As leaders, your mission is to create other high-quality leaders. In servant leadership, you mentor others and guide them in high-quality principles. Information shared within this process is specific to the mentee's needs. As an evolving leader, find someone you want to model his or her leadership style and develop a relationship. This will be the best person for your journey. High-quality mentoring greatly enhances your chances of success.

What is mentoring?

Mentoring is a process of growth and development from one person to another. The mentor provides guidance or knowledge through intelligence, skills, or experiences with the mentee, who is the less experienced individual.

Throughout my career, I have met several mentors in my professional life. These individuals can be your personal board of directors. As a consistent influence, I have had my immediate manager, Jeff, who has fostered my development from a brand-new manager into my role today as clinical director over the largest client in our book of businesses. He has provided high-quality, constructive feedback and guided my path of newfound management knowledge. Do you have anyone you would consider as a mentor?

Mentors should have a genuine interest in your professional development. They should exhibit mindful listening skills and coach you on a path of solutions. The individual must retain your confidence and be committed to your success. Hopefully, you are having someone come to your mind. Mentoring benefits the organization, individuals, and mentors.

Skills of a mentor:

1. Open-mindedness

2. Mindful listening

3. Inquisitiveness

4. Honesty

5. Self-awareness

For the organization, there are many benefits to having mentors. These include knowledge transfer, structured learning, identifying high potential individuals, fostering an organizational culture, and fine-tuning soft skills.

For the mentor, the benefits include building relationships, supporting and driving innovation, increasing professional contacts, enhancement of coaching skills, and personal satisfaction.

For the identified mentee or mentored individual, benefits include developing a new skill of guiding others. They gain professional growth, an in-depth understanding of the organization and culture, and the potential to mentor in the future.

Is reverse mentoring the future of leadership development?

The millennial generation has generated disruptive innovation throughout every organization known today. Millennials have brought technology, new expertise, and new viewpoints to the corporate table. Without innovation, the organization would fail.

Reverse mentoring is a new process of flipping top-down learning into a system where junior-level team member mentors a senior-level executive. Companies are discovering new innovative ways of leveraging social media and technology. This style of mentoring bridges the gaps between both individuals. These senior mentors learn about new technology and culture. The junior mentor has a role model and a career coach.

The reverse mentoring relationship has become pivotal at cultural insensitivities. It has strengthened both generations of collaborative partnerships and advancing organizations.

Coaching

When is it necessary to use coaching? How do you know what to coach? Coaching is designed for behavioral changes. Consider behavioral changes as modifiable risk factors for a heart disease patient—aspects of the individual that is within his power to change.

There are situations in organizations when it becomes necessary to introduce coaching. Typically, performance and skill enhancements are the primary reasons a manager would coach an individual. This is a type of coaching that focuses on core skills that are required to carry out tasks and handle work responsibilities effectively. Skills coaching is targeted at improving the basic skills of an individual for the general well-being and growth of the company or establishment.

Some additional situations would include:

- **Change-management** coaching is implemented before a major change in the structure or work pattern within an organization. This helps to align the attitude and behavior of the individual with the new work structure and condition to optimize output. This would help everyone involved to adjust to the new changes and mentally process the changes.

Think back to when you had a concern about changes in leadership, such as a change in manager. The same concern or anxiety will happen to your team. Consider change as an opportunity for growth and convey this to the team. This is also an opportunity for you to lead through any disruption of your processes.

- **Career coaching** focuses on coaching the individual's career interests. Career coaching assesses the individual's career capabilities and helps him to adjust and improve his career output. It brings about a personal reevaluation of the career outlook and a development plan where the individual being coached emerges with more clarity in career awareness. This coaching helps the employee adapt to the change in his or her given role or work position within the organization.

- **Personal life coaching** focuses on people who are being coached on a very personal level. It explores their aspirations, needs, wishes, all they want to make of themselves, and all they need to make out of life. Personal or life coaching provides support for them to make changes that reposition them in life.

- **Team facilitation coaching** is conducted with the purpose of enhancing output for a particular goal of an organization. Team facilitation extensively improves self-confidence and the performance of a team in laying down strategies and execution of tasks.

In the clinical setting, this would be providing strategic direction to the care team. For example, 30 percent of diabetic patients are not in control of their diabetes. The new focus is driving better glucose control in this population. Coaching would include discussing with the team on how to achieve diabetic disease management control.

- **Shortage of talents**: When an organization runs into the dilemma of a shortage of team members in manning special positions, a cheaper and more cost-effective approach is to coach the current team. This intervention would develop their skills and make them capable of manning whatever position is available.

Now that you have identified when to coach, let's focus on the fundamentals of coaching.

In today's workplace environment, coaching has dominated as the most effective means of engagement. Coaching is an ongoing interactive process that leads individuals to discover insights, take ownership, and develop actionable goals on performance and development. Engagement through insights leads to sustainable change. The individual isn't broken or of less intelligence. Many times, individuals become obsessed with the present problem and lose sight of the lesson.

Coaching is designed as a mechanism for learning lessons from past experiences and creating self-discovery to modify future outcomes. Understanding when coaching would not be effective is important for every leader. Mental illness, legal policy violations (harassment), family-dynamic changes, and state of emergency crises are better left to professionals and a consultation with your human resources representative (HBR Guide to Coaching Employees, 2015). It is also critical not to turn a coaching session into a blame game or gripe session.

As a servant leader, it is also important to realize that everyone can benefit from coaching. As someone who is focused on serving others, you are in a unique position to recognize employees with potential. You can spot team players and those who are capable of more. Use your desire to serve to help them become better employees. Coach them to help them develop their own skills.

Setting the scene

Coaching is essential to developing a growth mindset, which is vital to the success of you and your team.

Any coaching session requires preparation! Be open-minded and a mindful listener. Keep in mind a 4:1 ratio of listening to speaking. Any more than that, you are teaching and not coaching. Good coaches know their own biases and how the individual fits into the big picture. A *great* coach will develop while guiding the company's missions and goals.

While coaching, be mindful of your presence and keep the acronym STOP in mind:

- <u>S</u>low speech
- <u>T</u>one of voice: lower-than-normal speaking voice
- <u>O</u>pen questions and posture
- <u>P</u>ause for active listening and eye contact

Creating a thriving environment will instill confidence, thus leading to positive changes in performance. Also, for effective coaching, you must have a connection with the individual. Caution yourself not to fix the problem. Keep in mind that your team member is not broken.

How do you know when to coach? Coaching is designed for behavioral changes. Think of these as modifiable risk factors or things that we have the power to change. Aspects of the individual that is within his or her power to change would include weight, diet, exercise, response to a situation, etc.

A quick coaching method is leveraging the GROW model. Created by Sir John Whitmore and Graham Alexander in the 1980s. The model has several variations.

Let's look at each component of the GROW method to understand the implications:

Goals

For coaching, determine the long- and short-term goals. The long-term goal is changing the desired or targeted behavior. The short-term goals are goals for each coaching session. Remember that this coaching process will require more than one session.

Before coaching an individual, consider the goal of the coaching session. What would be the successful outcomes? What behavior do you want to see modified?

Consider your management goals surrounding what behavior you want to modify. Is it a modifiable behavior or an innate personality characteristic? Personality characteristics are not modifiable. However, these elements are the opportunity to facilitate an individual's understanding of how others perceive their traits.

For example, have you encountered an individual who says, "I know I am/can be____ (fill in the blank)"? While this is an innate characteristic, the individual recognizes that it can be a challenge for others.

Now, consider reasonable goals for the individual being coached. Their insights should lead them to a personal goal that achieves the manager's long-term goal.

When setting goals, make them **SMART**:

S=Specific: what has to be achieved?

M=Measurable: how do you determine your success?

A=Achievable: what steps will you take?

R=Relevant: can you describe your perfect world?

T=Time-bound: when do you see yourself reaching your goal?

Consider the goals, make them SMART, and write them down.

Reality

You will ask open-ended questions that lead to describing the situation objectively. Consider the most common and use the individual's own words:

What do you mean by_____?

Anything else?

Could you tell me more about_____?

Leveraging one of these three top questions will provide an open avenue for conversations, eliminate your personal bias, and avoid possibly interjecting your own conclusions into the situation. Practice the questions in role-play with a colleague. Say each question more slowly than your regular tone and in a slightly deeper tone. Notice how the person responds. This will create a calming environment and provide a more comfortable and defused atmosphere to discuss the situation.

Ensure that you are leveraging your active listening skills to focus on what and how the situation is being described. The team member will tell you everything you need to know if you just listen. Continue with the discussion until the individual has insight.

Options

The options step is devised to elicit insights specific to solutions for the problem. Think of this as the brainstorming session. Have the individual leverage personal insights to guide themselves toward a solution. What are their thoughts about solving the problem? While your goal is to elicit insights, some individuals may need a suggestion to start the process as this will probably be awkward for them during the first session.

Consider these questions to elicit insight:

What could have been done differently?

What if nothing is done?

What challenges and obstacles are you likely to encounter?

What will be the first step you make?

Will

In the will stage, you will guide in the choice of one of the options and create an action plan similar to a treatment or care plan for a patient. You will need to assess the motivation of the team member.

Consider these questions to guide the conversation:

Which options work best for you?

How will you start?

What obstacles will you encounter?

How will you overcome the obstacles?

When shall we meet again to check your progress?

As the plan emerges, write it down. Ask the individuals how they will hold themselves accountable as well as the preferred frequency for you to hold them accountable.

After the coaching session, provide follow-up support. This will be a new process for them and when they need you most. This is where they will test the options and will of the GROW model. There will be obstacles and possible confusion. This is another opportunity for coaching. If you always provide the answer, folks will always line up at your door needing an answer.

Opportunities to Express Leadership Abilities

You might have and portray great leadership abilities but lack avenues to exert them. In such instances, you will be required to find ways through which you can influence people with your leadership abilities without authority. As opposed to the old days when you could influence people even with minute authority positions, the current era requires us to focus on ways through which we can create avenues that we can use to influence people with our leadership abilities. Currently, people work with each other. Many organizations embrace the teamwork method of running their affairs. Thus, if you have leadership skills, but you lack the best affirmative ways to exert them, you might not impact people with such roles. You might not unleash your abilities.

The best thing in the current times is the fact that dependency is eliminated, unlike the old days. The current leadership styles require no hierarchy systems. This chapter gives you an opportunity to get some ways through which you can exert your leadership abilities despite your career or rank in the organization that you belong to. **The following are some of the ways you can influence without any authority** (Stoner, 2012):

1. Character

A person's character is a great source of influence. Are you a leader by example? Remember you cannot be a good leader by imposing commitments in your life but failing to follow them. The best way is to work on ensuring that you follow all the commitments that you make in life. Ensure that you have met all the promises that you make in your life. In this way, those people who emulate you will be able to follow your good traits, thereby accepting your leadership roles in their life. You should be trustworthy, authentic, and respectful. Respect comes with respect. The way you handle other people with respect is the way they reciprocate your actions with respect for you. This improves both your self-esteem and the team's dignity. They will be able to recognize you and give you the opportunity to lead them. Those people who believe in you are motivated by the positive general traits that you portray in your life.

2. Expertise

You have got to have some experience in understanding what is required of you to become a leader. You have to understand the essential skills and expertise that are vital for you to lead. This can be achieved by you gaining some content knowledge as well as experience. You have to gain an understanding of the process that you require in order to accomplish certain objectives. Influence and leadership go hand in hand. Thus, you need to have clear logic and proper explanation of the benefits of your leadership. Be assured that when taking a step to gain expertise in experience and knowledge of leadership, you unleash your abilities to impact the leadership skills on others.

3. Information

The other way through which you can create a leadership position that can easily be used with other people is through creating databases for information. If you have access to information, this is the best way to influence others. The only thing that you should put into consideration is ensuring that the information and data are valuable and applicable to the real-life situation. In this case, you should provide both the information and its source.

4. Connectedness

In this case, you should work on ensuring that you form close relationships with people. Have you ever stayed with a group/team of people from different educational and social backgrounds? Do such people enjoy working with you? Do they recognize your presence? This is the best way to engender the loyalty of such a big team of people. Always ensure that you have improved your connection with them. Influence them by portraying values that are positive, whether emotional or shared.

5. Social Intelligence

This is yet another avenue that you can use to unleash your leadership skills. If you have ever found yourself offering solutions that assist people in resolving certain issues, then you can be a great leader through this avenue. Leaders are depicted with the ability to provide sound solutions to various problems. They are depicted as offering people positive thoughts and insights that assist them in solving interpersonal problems that interfere with their work or life. Through such qualities, people will believe that you will be able to assist them in working together effectively.

6. Network

Placing the appropriate individuals in touch with one another is a great way to establish proper networks. You should be able to garner the proper endorsements of people who are credible. In this way, people will end up offering you the support needed for you to become their leader. Networking is a great tool to improve who you are by unleashing your leadership capabilities and exerting them on other people. This improves their general lives and provides motivation to head to the next level.

7. Collaboration

Just like networking, collaborating with like-minded individuals so that you can seek win-win solutions is a great avenue to exert your leadership capabilities. If you work toward building the community with a unified coalition, then collaboration is the best way to go. Through collaboration, people begin to trust that you can help them. By entrusting themselves to you, they give you a chance to lead them. This works as the best way of motivation if used appropriately.

8. Funding

If you have good access to financial support, then you have a great avenue to lead people. This is also true if you have the skills need to fundraise large amounts of money. Most issues in the world require finances, and thus people will offer your support for leadership as long as you can respond with financial support.

Before thinking about how you can lead people, it is good to ensure that you have built your leadership muscles by improving your leadership skills. This will give you the ability to use them in times of need. In this case, the muscles are the leadership traits that you are required to have for people to recognize you as their leader. Be the best example and they will follow you!

Chapter 3: Principles of Servant Leadership

Etiquette

Leadership is a science; it is about developing a hypothesis, setting an aim, collecting the resources, and methodically taking action. Once the leadership action is complete, we analyze our results, draw conclusions, learn, and gain an understanding of what the next steps are.

Leadership is also an art. It requires awareness to understand the context (the canvas). It requires a trust in our ability to draw on all of our experience (how we hold the brush) and conviction that the action we are about to take, provided it is done with care, is right for that moment (the brush strokes that go toward making the picture).

The Etiquette of Leadership is the science and art of moving oneself or others to action. The Etiquette of Leadership is the art and science of leading well. It is the act of accomplishing a change in state in another or in a situation that could not have occurred but for our good leadership.

The principles that underlie the Etiquette of Leadership are the same as for etiquette—respect, considerateness, and truthfulness—and they are all evident in servant leaders (Mayne, 2019).

Servant leaders who excel are those who skillfully and sincerely apply understanding in their interactions with others.

The Etiquette of Leadership captures the wisdom of years of studying what makes for effective leadership. There are some common threads with the ordinary understanding of leadership, which will support you as you understand and master them. There is also something totally unique about the Etiquette of Leadership; it is entirely unique for each active leader. The etiquette of your leadership shares many aspects of ordinary leadership in common with other effective leaders.

It will also be your unique expression of who you are as a leader and how you exercise the Etiquette of your Leadership efficiently. As you practice the Etiquette of Leadership and take on the attitudes that underpin it, you will increasingly be able to see their impact in the conventional practices that good leaders exhibit. You will also see it for your own leadership in the effects which your particular approaches have on yourself and others.

Principle 1: Respectful leadership is what works.

Respect is demonstrating your admiration for someone's abilities, qualities, or achievements. Respectful leaders are also respectable, i.e. they establish the conditions that allow others to offer them their respect. Consider the impact of being respectful of yourself and others.

In their consideration of others, respectful leaders take on the mantle of putting themselves in the other person's shoes before they act. They consider the other. They respect the position, person, and place of the other, just because they can. Their approach reflects the words of an old song, "Before you criticize and choose, walk a mile in my shoes."

Being respectful is a precondition for the practice of standard etiquette in life. It is part of being civil and living in a civil society. Leadership literature is replete with stories of apparently successful leaders who do outwardly unusual things at the expense of their followers, customers, and other stakeholders—even society as a whole. There is an increasing trend toward this kind of disrespectful incivility in organizational life. It is not acceptable to act on the basis that because a person has regulatory power over another, they have the ability or even the right to act in ways that diminish others.

Respect for self and others has the most profound impact on who one is as a leader. Respectful leadership is what flows when we have a good grasp of the first tenet of the Etiquette of Leadership, *you matter*, and the theme we developed in that tenet, *it's not about you*. When we understand ourselves and our true relationship with those we seek to lead, and when we focus on them and not ourselves, we are in a place of great potential to crystallize the power of being respectful of others.

Here is a short story to illustrate the effect of the Etiquette of Leadership practiced poorly.

"In my early days as a manager and an individual who leaders in the organization regarded as having career potential, I allowed myself to be seduced by the idea that because I had been promoted to a senior role as a very young person, I was, therefore, a 'someone.'

There were obviously some good things I was doing to have others form a favorable opinion of me. But in my quieter moments of reflection (such as they were in a callow youth!), I recognized that there were things I was doing that seemed to be off-key with others.

In my arrogance and ignorance, one particular practice that came up for me was that of taking reams of papers from my in-tray to meetings. These were materials that usually had no relationship with the meeting subject at all. As the meeting progressed, I would plow through papers; noting, approving, forwarding, or marking to be filed. I noticed that many of my meeting colleagues seemed puzzled by all this frenzied behavior, but I consoled myself with the idea that I could make productive use of my time by doing this stuff and still having the smarts to keep an ear on the conversations and discussions and make timely inputs.

I even used to do this during presentations by others where they would be standing at the front of the room, sometimes momentarily distracted by me shuffling papers and even distributing them to relevant others at the table.

Would you describe this as exercising the Etiquette of Leadership? To my shame, I later saw how disrespectful it was, to the chair of the meeting, to my colleagues, and to presenters. The Etiquette of Leadership requires leaders to be fully attentive, respectful of the norms of the situation, showing respect to other meeting participants and presenters, fully participating in conversation and deliberation on the subjects for the meeting."

Respect sits alongside being considerate and includes being thoughtful, caring, and even loving. It involves the notion of courtesy, the practice of polite behavior, and courtliness. This is an area where the Etiquette of Leadership might factor in your experience. The etiquette of your leadership should be much more than being polite because politeness can so often be a sword. The word *polite* comes from the same roots as *politics*. Even if you are a political leader, you do not want to exercise political politeness if you are seeking to practice the Etiquette of Leadership. If you do, you will be acting, not living. You will be using the Etiquette of Leadership as a means to a political end. In so acting, you will deny the opportunity to be genuinely respectful in your leadership. By behaving that way, you will create a world that is about you and not about others.

Respectful leadership also allows no room for us as the leader to manufacture subordination. The leader who expects to use the Etiquette of Leadership as a tool to create subordinates will fail.

There is an excellent piece of Australian history that illustrates this point above. In the early years of the colonization of Australia by the British, Governor Lachlan Macquarie distinguished himself as a builder, a promoter of social good and economic advancement. His great flaw was that he required and demanded that every other person in the colony be subordinate to him. It eventually led to his undoing. All his good acts were diminished because of a sense by those he sought to influence through his governorship that they had to regard themselves as under his authority.

This is an area where management can become contaminated by ineffective leaders who are not practicing the Etiquette of Leadership. Many managers act as if they are little gods. This is very often a result of the manager as a leader having a poor grasp of their own identity as a leader and misunderstanding the complicated relationship between their own sense of self and the respect that others deserve from them as leaders and managers.

Managers and leaders who adopt command and control approaches, who act politically, and who operate from their position inappropriately all serve to diminish the respect that their followers want to give them but do not because these actions promote fear, discomfort, unease, and even sickness. When they act superiorly, they place themselves, their opinions, ideas, and intelligence above others in ways that diminish.

One of the great ways that we can build respect *from* others is to show respect *to* others. One of the wonderful ways to undertake this is through the simple act of acknowledgment. By acknowledging someone's abilities, qualities, or achievements, we are merely showing that person that we see them. As described in the example above, a leader with followers he or she regards as subordinates drags behind them a tethered mass of disrespect of their own creation. In the process of acknowledgment, a leader demonstrates their respect and connects with the individuals within their followership, allowing them to move to their highest point, inadvertently taking the leader and the rest of the followership with them.

Another way to build respect and to keep your own ethical edge sharp is to consider whether you should always speak respectfully about others. If you choose to take this on as a sound practice, you are likely to notice that it builds respect for you. When we hear a leader speaking disrespectfully about others, it often makes us uneasy. This is not only because of what is being said disrespectfully about the other person. It can also cause us to think fearfully about what that same leader might be saying disrespectfully to others about us. In the process of so doing, leaders practicing poor Etiquette of Leadership damage their own sense of respect. This process can become a vicious cycle.

In speaking respectfully of others and in seeking to acknowledge others, there is some risk of appearing to be dishonest and untruthful. You will need to think this through for yourself. Our approach, as a piece of advice that you can consider and choose to follow or ignore as you desire, is that it is always more beneficial to speak respectfully about others. If we have to make *negative* assessments of others to third parties, we seek to confine statements to those that are relevant to solving an issue, not in gratuitously attacking the other person's character and reputation.

The Etiquette of Leadership acts as a guide for you as a leader in the ways you can demonstrate respect. Following it allows you to optimize your desire as a servant leader to benefit others.

It also serves another purpose: It facilitates the propulsion of the followership. By this, we mean that respectfulness creates alignment and unity so that those following you yearn to be in action. Often the actions that your followers undertake will be propelled and accelerated because your followers will derive new energy.

At this point, we encourage you to reflect.

Before we conclude this piece, it is worthwhile focusing for a moment on how you apply the Etiquette of Leadership when someone you seek to lead breaches your understanding of what constitutes either common etiquette or the Etiquette of Leadership itself.

Say, for example, that you are leading a project to build a new structure. You have been working long hours, and pressure to finish the project is mounting. In a project review meeting, one of the team members begins to speak angrily about the delays they allege have been caused by another team member.

Your capacity to respond as a leader exercising your unique Etiquette of Leadership skills gets to be tested right there. In many ways, this is the sort of situation that defines the Etiquette of Leadership and allows you to demonstrate your personal mastery of it.

What would you do in that situation? What would you say? Would you have confidence that the outcome of whatever happens next will lead to further productivity for the project team?

We leave this with you as a thought-starter to bring home the immensely practical implications of this work for you in designing and practicing the Etiquette of Leadership for your own situation.

Principle 2: Considerate Leadership is what makes a difference.

Leaders exercising consideration in their Etiquette of Leadership intentionally create the conditions for others to do their best in response to the call or the situation requiring action.

We do this by being mindful of the state that the others are in and what we as the leader assess is going to be needed to bring effectiveness. That awareness or mindfulness can be gained through our senses and also our intuition. Here is an example.

Joyce is walking toward a group of people. She sees them milling around. She hears voices being raised. Some appear to be acting provocatively toward others. One person is lying on the ground. The movements of the group are staccato, abrupt. She senses there is anxiety, anger, upset. The situation looks potentially explosive; punches may start to be thrown any minute.

All these responses she has are considerations. She considers them. They may or may not be accurate since they are conclusions she has come to or possibilities she has entertained about the meaning of the situation. Whether she has accurately assessed the situation or not, she decides to act considerately.

She moves closer to the group. She listens. She hears one person speaking apparently aggressively to another. The rest of the team seem to be bystanders, although some appear to be egging the aggressive person on. A couple of others are acting defensively, protectively toward the person experiencing the aggression.

Joyce moves closer, standing to the right of the aggressive person and potentially between what looks to be the two protagonists. She breathes in, aware of her own body position, calling on her inner resources to stay calm. She consciously lowers her speaking pitch and puts out her hand at waist level, palm down. She begins to speak and slowly moves further forward.

All these gestures and insights are part of her considerate leadership.

She has prepared herself for leadership by being considerate.

We can't know what the outcome of that situation will be, but we can be assured that her consideration of all the aspects leading up to her action has been made considerately. It is our contention that this makes a huge difference to the effectiveness of leadership at the moment. It is an example of the essence of the Etiquette of Leadership.

Considerate leadership also gives keen attention to the safety of the other, as well as the self. This includes both physical and emotional safety. Leadership can be exercised in unsafe moments. However, they are much more likely to have beneficial outcomes if the safety of self and others is maximized in the situation at hand and in the thoughts the leader is having about what will happen next.

Considerate leadership allows the other to be free; free to act, think, respond, reply, build, connect, or a thousand other responses. Freedom to react is a crucial part of considerate leadership. We allow others to process and respond to our direction by creating permission, permission for the other to be free. Our contention is that this freedom creates the opportunity for generative leadership. By this, we mean the transformational outcomes that occur when real leadership creates a useful and forward momentum in others that accomplishes that which would not otherwise have happened without that leadership.

Considerate leadership has almost, but not quite, no place for a desire to control. It may be a desire to control others or to control a situation. It gives off the idea that the leader is the only one who can determine what is morally right or wrong in a situation and that therefore the leader is justified in taking away the freedom to act. This is not part of the Etiquette of Leadership.

Followers will usually work and respond best to your leadership when you speak and act in such ways that your followers are released, enabled, feel respected, and encouraged to move forward. The only exception we know of where control is sometimes the best form of considerate leadership is where the followers lack capability or competence to do what the situation requires. Then, the leader may need to direct and control.

The significant risk in always acting and speaking in a controlling or directing way is that it brings the focus of attention to the leader. If you choose to take that quality on as part of your Etiquette of Leadership, so be it. We find that the risks of ego, narcissism, and the like becoming dominant usually outweigh the possible benefits, but we encourage experience, accompanied by reflection with the intention to learn from that experience. As we said above, sometimes this is necessary, but it is more likely to happen in situations such as where your followers lack competency, or there is a real emergency.

It is also likely that leaders who habitually seek to control others lack care. Sometimes it is masked in paternalistic thoughts and ideas. But it is usually tough to be a controlling leader and at the same time to be a caring leader, to exercise respect and esteem, and to speak and act in such ways that you do not make others fearful because of your attention to their frailties and shortcomings.

If you think about situations where you have operated in this way or have experienced leaders who have acted in this way toward you, you will notice that this behavior creates dependency. It forces the creation of adult/child relationships, which might be appropriate if the leaders were an adult and the follower was a child. It is an approach that is unlikely to be effective in the longer term between two adults or a leader and a group of adults.

A useful adjunct to this idea above occurs when we, as leaders exercising the Etiquette of Leadership, realize the power to be had as a leader when we speak and act so as not to make the other feel or consider themselves wrong, lacking, falling short, or not being up to the mark. Situations may create these conditions—people never do. Or, at least the other needs to be assured that the situation has resulted in an unfavorable state but no matter how bad it is, the person, himself, is not *wrong*. They might see for themselves that they need to change or make other decisions to affect the situation. But real leadership is most likely to occur when the focus is on the situation to be addressed, not on the innate quality of the other as a person.

Considerate leadership happens when we act so elegantly that the response of others is to be drawn to us, seeking to do what we propose or agree with what we say, or at least give it consideration. The Etiquette of Leadership does not hold room for creating an impression in what we say and do that the other must do something to win our favor or come up to our standard as access to having our acceptance. We do not hold to the idea that embarrassment, belittlement, isolation, and the like are acceptable approaches in the Etiquette of Leadership. We hold to the idea that our behaviors are most likely to be focused on creating *we* rather than *I* and *you*.

Now that you have read this far it may appear to you that the ideas of respect and consideration seem to overlap—they do. There are also some differences. Respect is essentially about valuing the other person for who they are. Consideration is about appreciating their situation. When we exercise the Etiquette of Leadership considerately, we are considering the circumstances of the situation that we find ourselves in. We are applying our awareness. We are continuing to take in and process the signals. We recall the important pieces of data about ourselves, others and the situation that will allow us to act effectively.

Then when we speak or act, we are doing so with consideration. That is the essence of a servant leader. They strive to lead in such a way that those around them benefit. There is no way that your team members wouldn't benefit from respect and consideration.

At this stage, it is essential to note that when considering a person or group's situation, care needs to be exercised to know the fine line of passing judgment. A considerate leader will put themselves in somebody else's shoes to gain an understanding of their situation. The Etiquette of Leadership takes the leader a step further.

When gaining an understanding of someone's situation, it is important not to make a judgment about that situation—things are where they are. This is the element that creates freedom within your consideration for others. As a leader practicing the Etiquette of Leadership, the next step you take is to determine how your actions can create a safe experience that allows that person to grow.

In addition to being considerate about the circumstances that have led up to the moment of leadership and the present moment itself, we also are considerate of the future. What could be the outcomes of our words and actions in exercising leadership? What will the impact be for others and ourselves?

Much of the commentary about the practice of leadership focuses on the outcomes in terms that do not include the impact of our words and actions on the state of others. The focus is often on getting the job done with little or no thought as to the overall impact on others. When we act considerately with the Etiquette of Leadership, we are deliberate and give conscious consideration to where the others are going to be left emotionally, physically, and spiritually by our words and actions of leadership.

We may not be able to predict or control the impact on others in advance. All the planning and thought we can possibly do is unlikely to always and forever determine the outcome. But the process of giving consideration can improve the likelihood of effective outcomes.

Our impact can be so much more significant if it is considered in advance. It can also be more significant at the moment if we are consciously paying attention as we are moving our lips or exercising our muscles in leading. Paying attention, being aware, and considering others can allow us to make small or large alterations to our delivery at the moment to increase our effectiveness.

We have a mission with regard to exercising the Etiquette of Leadership with consideration. We can know that we are leading considerately when we see that we are operating and others are responding, and the overall effect is that leadership is being exercised with no harm. This is a crucial element in acting with consideration.

To circle back to earlier material, leading with a conscious consideration of seeking to do no harm involves respect and ethical dealings. It also reflects your desire to act wisely. As a servant leader, you cannot entirely prevent damage, but it should always be your aim to ensure no harm is done, so far as you humanly can.

There are great warrior stories of impassioned leadership speeches, such as those that occur in wartime. You can imagine the scene where the leader is about to sound the charge to battle, and he rallies the troops ready to go over the top of the trenches and off to almost certain death. These situations do occur. But except in the most arduous times of war, they do not happen in reality, even in the armed forces, except in the most exceptional circumstances. Today, modern military leaders spend enormous amounts of time and effort planning to ensure that no harm is done in action. This quality of consideration gives troops in war a heightened sense of respect and trust, knowing that their leaders have considered every possible factor to ensure no harm comes to them builds their faith in their leaders.

If this is the case in theaters of war where real physical harm and even death can occur, how much more relevant is it in modern workplaces? Good leaders do not trifle with their followers' safety. They always seek to ensure that no harm is done as a result of actions that have to occur.

When we are planning a leadership act, especially regarding a significant matter that will impact on our followers' lives, we owe it to them to plan to do no harm. If our leadership actions have repercussions for others' emotional and physical safety, we are obligated and motivated to prepare thoroughly to minimize the adverse results.

So far, much of this section has been focused on considering others. We can do ourselves a great service too as leaders if we give consideration to ourselves—the impact of what we say and do on ourselves.

Much of the present dysfunction that occurs in organizations today can be directly attributed to the failure of leaders to be considerate to themselves. This is not a call for giving managers more money or larger offices, it is more so that good leaders know the impact of their leadership on their own emotions. They act considerately of themselves by engaging in activities such as enlarging their emotional intelligence, practicing awareness training, debriefing with a competent coach or another professional support person, or even rewarding themselves for a period of high performance with some extra sleep rather than merely continuing at a frenetic pace.

At this point, we encourage you to reflect.

Here is an excellent test of whether you are exercising this tenet of consideration in your practice of the Etiquette of Leadership; notice how you respond to others who display some kind of weakness. It might be a physical weakness, it might be a weakness of intellectual grasp, or it might be something as simple as the weakness of another in not knowing what to do in a particular situation. If you act graciously, generously, understandingly, and considerately, you should notice that you create a much better likelihood of moving a situation forward than if you do not. This is a real moment of leadership, what you do in the face of another's weakness.

If you are exercising consideration as part of your Etiquette of Leadership, the other person keeps breathing regularly and deeply into their stomach; if they continue to feel safe and that you have been considerate of them, they will tend to breathe low.

What do you notice with yourself when you are considerate and when you are not?

Principle 3: Truthful leadership is what endures

In the writings of etiquette teachers, you will see their reference to the importance of honesty in etiquette. The good host is said to be able to speak honestly about a situation and also always uphold the other tenets of etiquette.

In the Etiquette of Leadership, we have redefined and sharpened this idea. Some bad leaders would take the concept of honesty and use it as an excuse for poor speaking or conduct. Being *honest* can easily be misused as an excuse for being brutal or hurtful of the other.

Our conception of this principle is enlarged to add truthfulness to honesty. Someone speaking honestly speaks earnestly, deliberately, keeping to the facts and the like. Someone speaking truthfully speaks what is true. There are many philosophical distinctions regarding the notion of truth. We intend it to mean something quite specific here. By *truth*, we mean being sure, as designed, as planned, right, ringing true. Some would include the distinction of *integrity* as another way of describing truth as we are outlining it here. We say that truth in the Etiquette of Leadership encompasses all these elements.

We have purposefully listed truth thirdly in the list of principles because the truth is powerful and it needs to be supported by respect and consideration to have a real and positive impact. Without the other two principles in the mix, damage and devastation can be left in the wake of truth. When, as a leader, you stand in the truth of the situation there is power; it is the simplicity of truth that gives it its power. No one can whittle it away; it doesn't need your justification; it can just *be*. Even though there is a simplicity to the truth, the important thing is how it is delivered, and this is where respect and consideration come into play.

The old saying *truth hurts* doesn't have to be right. An influential leader, with experience of the Etiquette of Leadership, will know how to deliver truth and demonstrate its power graciously that will lead to the follower-ship emulating the practice.

We also add another element to our conception of truth in the Etiquette of Leadership. It is acting in such a way that the other will respond to our leadership with trust and fidelity. The greatest moments of leadership occur when we lead and others respond by putting their trust and confidence in us. This is an enormous privilege granted in the moment of truly effective direction, and it comes with how the power of truth is being handled. The trust exhibited by those who follow our leadership is code for them feeling secure in what we have said or done or propose to do.

In that moment of trust, another great thing happens—others give us their fidelity. Fidelity is an old word connoting loyalty and faithfulness. Dogs are said to be paradigms of loyalty to their owners. We don't want to create situations where followers act obediently and ingratiatingly toward us. We want them to respond with a great and genuine sense that what we are leading them about can best be responded to with their honest and enduring support. When that happens, they will be confident in the outcome we are leading them toward. In that circumstance, they are willing to give us their trust.

Good leaders practicing the Etiquette of Leadership, speak and act truthfully. We say what is so. We go where we intend to go. We move as planned.

Our words and actions bring truth. In speaking and acting truthfully, we reinforce the tenets of respect and consideration. They all combine to bring progress and advancement to a situation.

At this point, we encourage you to reflect.

When practicing the Etiquette of Leadership, what does it feel like for you to speak and act truthfully?

Can you recall a time when you have acted against the truth in an attempt to achieve the desired outcome, appease someone, or simply disregard the potential impact of taking this action? What happened? What were the levels of respect and consideration received from your followership? If you still received the same degree of respect and consideration, how did that make you feel?

There are times when many of us feel or think little about those "white lies" or sentiments of "what people don't know won't hurt them," but practicing the Etiquette of Leadership is not only about that one moment. It is also about a journey of mastery; it is not only about your journey, but it also includes those of your followership, those you interact with, and those that come after you.

Respect, consideration, and truth are fundamental principles that will help keep the pathway of your journey clear. If you genuinely want to be a servant leader, following the Etiquette of Leadership will allow you to know best how to interact with those you lead.

Chapter 4:
Overcoming the Harsh Reality of Organizational Life with Strong Leadership

Managing Workplace Conflict

If you own or manage a practice and haven't had to deal with a toxic employee yet, just wait—you eventually will. If toxic employees are not confronted early, they can quickly poison the well and bring a lot of damage. These employees hurt morale, disrupt the workplace, and cause other team members to be less engaged with their work and ultimately less productive. Toxic employees almost always create some level of workplace conflict.

The steps below will focus on confronting toxic employees who cause or exasperate workplace conflict ("Managing Workplace Conflicts," 2018).

5 Steps to Managing Workplace Conflict

Identify the issue

Awareness starts with shining a spotlight on the issue. However, it's essential to do this in a manner that does not evoke immediate defensiveness. "I would like to talk with you about your communication style" will be better received than "I would like to speak with you about your bad attitude." Use broad, benign terms like "communication style" or "leadership" and avoid negative terms or specific situations such as "I want to talk to you about how you acted yesterday at our staff meeting." This instantly places people on the defensive and lessens the chance of a positive outcome.

Describe the impact it has on the team

Workplace conflict can become an incredible distraction for employees. Conflict and dispute in the workplace can become a major time sucker that allows less time to focus on getting real work done. The practice can't move forward. You find yourself just spinning your wheels trying to get through another day without any major fires popping up. Explain how the conflict is affecting teamwork and morale. You may even be able to demonstrate this with declining sales numbers, higher turnover, or negative patient reviews. Rick needs to understand *WHY* this has to change.

Acknowledge your contribution

As a manager and leader, it's possible that you have contributed to the problem by allowing it to go unchecked for too long. Perhaps you've failed to address conditions that could have averted the problem. Maybe you have not clearly spelled out responsibilities and expectations—leading to confusion and power struggles among the staff. Workplace conflict is much more likely to flourish in an undermanaged environment. Acknowledging any contributions on your part will be well received by the employee(s) and let them know that you are more interested in a solution than a reprimand. It is vital that you begin to fill this leadership vacuum immediately to avoid similar problems in the future.

Ask for solutions

Once the issue has been clearly identified for the employee along with a clear explanation of how it is impacting the workplace and why it needs to be resolved, engage the employee in a discussion of how to improve the situation. The entire conversation up to this point should not take long, maybe a minute or two. Move the conversation quickly toward solutions. If the employee wants to focus on negativity and accusations of other employees, steer the conversation back to solutions. Strongly indicate your wish to resolve the issue. Come to an agreement on how you are going to proceed and then reschedule a future meeting to review progress. As a manager, sometimes you need to hear both sides and make decisions that everyone will have to live with. The more engaged you are with the staff, the more likely you understand the situation.

Revisit the conversation

Even if you have presented the problem in a diplomatic manner, don't be surprised if the immediate reaction is denial or defensiveness. "It didn't occur in that way" or "it wasn't my fault" may be the response you hear. Don't go there with them. Just reiterate your desire to work toward a solution and offer to revisit the conversation in the coming days. It's normal to need a day or two for conversations like this to sink in. The follow-up conversation will offer greater insight into the individual's openness to behavior change and a positive outcome.

When to part ways: If the employee refuses to improve his or her behavior or even acknowledge there is a problem, it's best to part ways with this employee. Failure to remove a toxic employee who refuses to change will lead to a stressful, unhappy work environment. Service will suffer, and teamwork will decline. This won't go unnoticed by your patients.

Handling Change

Why is change difficult?

People often fear change because it is uncertain. The status quo feels comfortable and safe. In the face of change, employees often fear the idea of additional work, having to learn new systems or possibly even losing their position or prestige within the practice. There is an emotional barrier that must be overcome. Managers often use a logical approach to deal with the practical elements of a change but ignore the emotional side of the equation. For change to "stick," this requires leadership to address the emotions that create barriers to change.

Why is change necessary?

The eye care industry and the health care industry as a whole are changing at rapid speed. Health care reform continues to evolve. Disruptive technologies that threaten the traditional practice of optometry continue to emerge. Low-cost competitors and online vendors are putting increased pressure on brick and mortar practices. How will you respond? What can you control? What are the competitive strengths that you can leverage in your market?

If your practice doesn't change and evolve, you are certain to get left behind. Yesterday's ways cannot be tomorrow's ways, and the ability to lead a team to change has never been more critical. Without goals and priorities, you are just maintaining the status quo.

5 Steps to Managing Change

Prioritize

Managers often fail to motivate employees to change because they move too fast or try to do too much at once. If you attempt to introduce too much change at once, staff will become overwhelmed and your initiatives will likely fail. A key to executing change in a business is keeping employees focused on what's important. If you asked your staff to tell you the top 3 priorities in practice and they don't have an answer, the reason is either because you have not set priorities, have set too many priorities, or have failed to clarify the top goals of the practice.

Research on human behavior consistently reveals that defining a small number of goals and priorities, maybe even one, and keeping a laser focus on accomplishing that goal improves the odds of success. While we like to believe we are good at multitasking, research suggests it's rarely an effective strategy. We end up shuffling between tasks, performance suffers, and stress levels spike. Devoting greater attention to fewer activities is a more practical approach.

Create a list of 6 or 7 goals you would like to accomplish in order of importance, and then focus your attention on the top 1 or 2. Keep moving down the list as you check off new accomplishments. Celebrate the wins with your team. The goal is steady and continuous improvement without overloading your staff.

Delegate

If the change calls for numerous responsibilities to be carried out simultaneously, then delegate smaller tasks to different employees. Change efforts in business often require a great deal of teamwork. This will require frequent meetings and coaching sessions with individual employees. Make sure each employee knows precisely what his or her role is in contributing to the defined objectives.

Clear the path

Your employees already have job responsibilities. If you are a busy practice, your employees are likely very busy as well. However, being "busy" does not always translate to being "productive," In many practices, waste and inefficiency are rampant. So much time is spent on routine tasks and activities that add little value to the training or patient experience that there is simply not enough time to execute changes necessary for growth. Efficiency gives you and your staff the time to focus on these changes. As a manager, you may have to clear the path for your team by challenging the manner in which things have been done all along. Look for ways to be more efficient. It's time to simplify and streamline.

Meet frequently

Ongoing feedback and communication are extremely valuable when implementing change in an organization. Failure of managers to keep a spotlight on these new initiatives will quickly lead to failure. Staff will abandon these changes in favor of the status quo. Managers must be persistent in communicating expectations to employees. They must continue to measure performance expectations and hold employees accountable. Make sure individual employees are clear on what is expected of them. Be concrete. Remove ambiguity and uncertainty from the process. Set specific goals and delegate responsibility. Track results. Use checklists. All of this will be reviewed and discussed at both staff and one-on-one meetings.

It's also important that staff understand why they are doing it. "Because I told you to" might work on children, but providing a meaningful rationale will be more effective on adults. Research shows that when people are given a meaningful rationale, they're more likely to invest more effort in the process and view their contributions as important. But not just any rationale will do. You have to show employees how the desired change will benefit them. Don't expect to get the full commitment of your staff if the change is perceived only to benefit the owner or bottom line.

Define the outcome, not the process

No individual is fond of the change imposed on them. One of my favorite business quotes is from Stephen Covey, the author of *The 7 Habits of Highly Effective People*. The quote is 4 words and easy to remember: "No involvement, no commitment." He is implying that without involving your employees in decisions, you will not have their commitment. People support what they create. You need the buy-in of your employees to develop momentum with new initiatives. If your staff does not support the change or feel involved with the process, they will become an obstacle to change. Not to mention, they may have great ideas or unique insight you had not considered. They stick to the front lines and see things that you don't. Your billing coordinator may have a solution to reduce your accounts receivable. Your millennial employees may have a better understanding of why more of your patients are ordering their glasses online. An authoritarian, non-collaborative environment would discourage this kind of discourse that could lead to innovative solutions.

When you meet with your workers or employees, cultivate an atmosphere of involvement. Ask for their ideas. Brainstorm solutions to problems and obstacles. Don't be afraid to get out of your way and try out new things and ensure you are ready to take risks. Give your staff permission and autonomy to try new ideas. If it doesn't work out, treat it as a learning experience and go back to the drawing board. When employees feel that they have no control over the work environment, motivation declines. Most successful organizations are a product of years of strategic trial and error. They repeat the successes and learn from the failures. Yes, it's essential that managers set clear expectations for staff, but employees can and should contribute their own ideas and solutions as well. An overemphasis on never failing or making mistakes restricts employee thinking and ignores a fundamental reality of how learning and innovation really happen. Creativity and unexpected solutions come through exploration, not settling into a routine. It's not just about your practice's performance today; it's about where your practice will be in 5 years.

Handle Firing People the Right Way

Everyone wants to know how to fire someone nicely or how to fire someone gracefully. I'm often asked, how do you fire a friend? How do you fire someone with dignity?

There is only one appropriate way to let someone go. It's the best way, whether you like the person or not.

Whether they are your friend, or you don't like them, whether you're firing them for poor performance or letting them go as part of a layoff, there is only one right way to give the news: **You need to do it quickly and directly (Grote, 2018).**

Step One: Tell Them

Make sure you are having the conversation in a private area, such as your office or a conference room with a closed door.

Your first sentence, after greeting them and asking them to sit, is to tell them they are being let go and that today is their last day. It may seem abrupt, but if you get that sentence out first the rest will go much easier, and the employee will have more time to absorb the news.

Step Two: Explain Why

Second, explain the reason why. Ideally, the person won't be surprised, and this isn't the time to get into a debate or argument or to rehash all the details. Just state the basic reason succinctly. You may say a statement like, "As you know, we've been having performance issues related to the number of typos that are going out in your emails."

Step Three: Explain Next Steps

Step three, explain what happens next regarding the exit process. The details will vary of course based on your organization. You might review:

- When will they receive their final paycheck (often, by law, it must be on the same day of termination)?

- What is included in the final paycheck (e.g., unused paid-time-off, commissions, etc.)?

- What happens to their health benefits? Do they qualify for continuation?

- Are you offering severance tied to a separation agreement?

Let them know that they'll probably have questions in the days and weeks ahead and they should contact you (or your HR department) at any time. Remember, anything you can do to reduce their anxiety will reduce the chances of them contacting a lawyer or file a wrongful discrimination lawsuit.

Step Four: Gathering Their Things

Next, depending on your company policy and the level of trust you have with the individual, you might explain that they will be escorted to gather their things, or you can meet them outside of regular work hours to pack up.

Remember, not only do they need to gather their personal belongings, they need to return any company property that might be in their possession.

Step Five: Questions

Ask them if they have any questions. Near the end, their minds may be reeling, so it's important to give them a minute to go over any points of confusion.

This is often the time when the employee will begin to probe further about the factors behind the termination. He might ask things like:

- How come I wasn't given more warning?

- Is this because I'm _____ (race, gender, age, religion, whatever)?

- Other people have made similar mistakes, so why am I the only one being fired?

While you want to clarify any potential misunderstandings, the termination meeting is not the right time or place to do so. This is the time when the employee's emotions will be highest, and they won't have had time to process the information given. Just answer any of these types of questions with something like, "I'm happy to talk again about the reasons for our decision but not at this time. If you want to schedule a time next week to talk again, that would be fine."

Step Six: Part on Good Terms

Finally, let them know that while it turned out the role wasn't right for them, you'd like to part on good terms. Let them know they can reach out with any questions in the days and weeks ahead. You could offer to make them aware of any open positions you come across and to reach out to your professional network for positions that might be a good fit for them.

While this extra step might not seem pleasant or necessary, you never know when a departing employee could end up working inside one of your client companies or may even become the client. And at the very least, think about your company's brand and what they'll tell family and friends about how they were treated.

In the past, I made the mistake of trying to be nice by not really saying *why* they were being let go. I was vague or told them it wasn't working out but it's the company's fault, anything I could do to make the other person not feel bad about himself. But it always backfired. Sometimes it dragged the process out longer. Sometimes they were confused. And if you're not direct with the person, you're actually robbing them of valuable feedback. This is feedback they can use to improve or at least find a job that fits their true strengths.

I've also made the mistake of agreeing to give the person just one more chance. They feel more stress than ever before, are now looking for another job as a backup, and the relationship between us is awkward. They always end up being fired anyway, or they resign once they land a new position.

And even in the best cases, they went away with valuable feedback—feedback that could lead them to a better next job, one that fits their talents better.

To fire someone nicely, just think about how you'd like to be treated if the roles were reversed. Realize that feedback can sometimes be painful, but it's always valuable.

- Be direct. The sooner you can say, "Hey, I'm sorry, but you're being let go and today is your last day," the better.

- Keep it short. Don't over-explain. If you just got that news, wouldn't you want to get out of the office as quickly as possible to process the whole thing and to begin to think of the next steps?

- Share the relevant next steps. Most people will want to know about their last paycheck, any commissions or unused paid time off, and how long their healthcare insurance last.

- Let them know you're there for them and want to remain friends in the future. The right way to be nice is after the termination. Return their phone calls and emails quickly in the days and weeks ahead as they have questions about things. Reach out to your professional network and see if anyone has an opportunity for this person. Just because they didn't work out in YOUR company or in that particular role doesn't mean they can't be successful somewhere else.

Conducting a termination is difficult, and it's harder when you like the person or if they've spent many years with the company. Just think about how you would like to be treated if the roles were reversed and let that be your guide.

Accept Others' Feedback

Just as you expect others to receive your feedback, you need to be willing to accept feedback from your employees or team members. If you want to serve others, then you need to understand how you can best serve them. They have needs that must be met, and even though you are trying to be an effective leader, you may not be serving them as they need.

Some companies use manager evaluations to collect feedback from employees. Others have a method in place to allow employees to give feedback anonymously. If your company doesn't have either, then consider setting aside time to talk to your employees yourself. Ask them how you can improve or what you should continue doing. Make sure they know they will not face any repercussions for their honesty. If they fear retaliation, then they will not be honest and asking for feedback will be pointless.

Receiving feedback, particularly negative feedback, is a time for growth. Don't view it as something negative about you; view it as a way to improve your own leadership qualities. After all, striving to be the best leader is part of being a servant leader.

Your Free Gift

As a way of saying thanks for your purchase, we're offering a free companion gift that's exclusive to readers of *Serve to Lead*.

With the companion gift, you'll discover a collection of updated recipes, checklists and useful bonus information that we couldn't fit into this book. Get the most out of this book, by getting the free companion here:

>> Go Here to Get The Free Serve to Lead Book Companion <<

https://www.book-companion.com/servant-leadership-book-companion

Would you like to listen to the Serve to Lead in your car? Get the **free Audible version** of this book on Audible.com. More information on the free promotion can be found on the companion website linked above.

Chapter 5:
Agile Project Management

Maybe you tried it a little or just heard rumors about Agile project management, but one thing is for sure, you cannot deny that a project manager is a superhero! Your customers expect their outcome within their budget and timeline. But then the requirements change again and again. This is such a common occurrence and a major reason you need to consider Agile project management over the unforgiving traditional approach. With Agile, even with a moving deliverable, you can still provide customers with precise status updates and hit important targets. This is possible because an Agile project manager gets consistent feedback, and the process is more visible ("Agile Project Management"). They can then respond faster to changes and problems in the process. This means the results are better and quicker.

What Is Agile?

Agile is more than a daily stand-up meeting. You cannot say your team is "Agile" until you truly understand what Agile is and what roles are required. Accepting change, providing high-quality work, giving current updates, controlling the budget, managing the timeline, and keeping the scope in perspective are all benefits of Agile ("Agile Project Management and Scrum"). This is drastically different from the older project management process that can end up being cumbersome, pricey, and prone to error. Previously, project management produced unreliable results until Agile.

Introduced in 1957, Agile project management, which is also referred to as iterative project management, lingered until 2001 (Varhol). The Agile Manifesto was released, and Agile became a hot topic, especially in the software development world. That's because this manifesto stressed working together and the need for a speedy response to change, which are the two complicated processes in traditional project management. Projects can be debilitated with delays that are long and costly, especially when a customer has waited to put the final touches on the project's expectations before getting your results. Being Agile puts you in the driver's seat, able to give your customers what they want when they want it, making you look stellar at the same time!

Instead of approaching a project as one complex entity that has phases to complete before the next begins, Agile allows you to break the project into small usable bits to be developed in a few weeks simultaneously, all leading to the final project. The timeline to complete a small portion typically takes no longer than four weeks. Traditional project management is complex, with a lengthy timeline, and is focused solely on the entire project. With Agile, you chunk up the project according to the broad ideas and allow the teams to design, create, construct, and assess their part before adding it to the whole. Another difference between Agile and traditional is that Agile has three roles to handle the responsibility instead of one.

The three roles of Agile include:

1. *Product Owner* - Sets project goals, navigates the scope versus the schedule for the trade-off, handles the changes to the project requirements, and develops the product features priorities.

2. *Scrum Master* - Assists the group with prioritizing tasks and eliminates challenges that affect their capability to ensure their tasks are complete. This is a new role for Agile.

3. *Team Members* - Complete tasks assigned to them, manage the details each day, reports on the progress made, and oversee the product quality control.

Concepts you may have also heard about like Kanban, Lean, and Scrum, are all methods for structured project management that were created from the concept of Agile. They each improved it in various ways, but ultimately the foundation from Agile is responsible for making them more successful in the completion of their projects.

Why Is Agile Important?

One of the most important sections of Agile project management is the ability to scrutinize and adjust. If you have tried Agile before and found it too hard, it is possible you were missing this part. When you include this function in your Agile, you will notice that every time you deliver a product, it only gets better and better. In addition, you can expect your customers to get better value from your team members' deliverables, and your company can expect the get more value from you.

The process of Agile incorporates an evaluation of cost and time, and it considers them the main constraint. To provide quality output and engage in established processes, your team's schedule is committed to giving immediate feedback developed with the intention of adapting constantly and a quality assurance protocol. Metrics are proactively delivered in real-time to Agile project managers through things like "Cumulative Flow," "Burndown," and "Velocity." This is instead of traditional project management Gantt charts, Excel spreadsheets, or ridiculous milestones. These changes are what makes Agile important to the success of your business; the faster completion time and fewer mistakes that pop up at the end, the less money it costs you.

The Scalability of Agile

Companies can fall into the trap of finding success with one Agile team and then creating more without a clear path for expansion. This common occurrence leads to a mixture of teams working independently with the tools that are not connected to the singular or clear vision of your company. The reason this occurs often is that scaling Agile is a difficult task that requires thought and follow-through. That being said, it can be done more efficiently using a few keys steps.

For example, a project manager, who knows from the beginning that one of the significant components of their job is balancing delivery with ROI, is paramount to the success of scalability. This means that the project manager must deliver the objectives on time by using a process that consistently operates at the lowest cost while providing the highest ROI. The best way to do this is to have Agile project management work with the Scrum team. This setup allows for an easily repeatable process that can be replicated across various projects and teams.

Repeating this process is also successful in alternative locations. An Agile project management team with Scrum creates a central location for all defects, tests, tasks, requests, and requirements and turns this knowledge into an invaluable tool. The team can now work together and make decisions without wasting time. The stakeholders can also receive the appropriate information for their needs precisely when it is needed.

The Strengths of Agile

The number one strength for Agile project management is the flexibility it offers. You can adapt the process to anything you need. This is one of the reasons it was used at the foundation for other systems, like Lean or Kanban. Boiling down the idea of Agile into the concept of chopping up your project into deliverable pieces that can be completed simultaneously allows you to modify the details to fit what you need.

The other strength of Agile is the priority of responsiveness to change over sticking to the plan. This again plays into the number one strength of flexibility; however, it is a distinct feature that sets Agile apart. You can deliver your product continually with a clear path and system to get you there.

The Weaknesses of Agile

As it typically occurs, the greatest strength is also its greatest weakness. Flexibility can result in a lack of attention and motivation to complete your project if you do not watch over it. Having a loose plan instead of milestones means there is no set process to check in on and see that there is a smooth progression. This looseness can result in the team losing focus. To combat this weakness, consider creating an internal process to run alongside Agile to help keep your teams on target, or consistently check in to ensure your teams are constantly communicating and moving onward. Sometimes you may even need to consider one of the offshoots of Agile if you continue to find this weakness tripping up your teams.

Agile vs. Traditional Methods

There is a vast difference between Agile project management and traditional project management; however, there are some important overlaps as well. No matter what form of project management a company employs, the purpose is the same: remove unnecessary glitches from the processes of their company. This vital role has made it a staple to the success of many businesses, so they can get their work done. It does not matter if the project management process is a traditional Waterfall method or Agile; the companies are after the same thing. So, no matter if the project is for managing a workflow or for time frames, the project management tool helps you keep moving forward with minimal disruption.

Despite the beauty of the possibility, there are limitations to the "magic" of project management. There are several approaches to project management, and many support the claim that Agile is the most flexible and practical tool available to companies now. Among many other clear advantages, Agile is able to support various projects.

Traditional Project Management Overview

You can apply project management to a variety of fields and projects. It is a global process with simple objectives and concepts. No matter if you are tackling a project intentionally or unintentionally, there is an element of management in it. When you use project management to complete your projects, you are following basic guidelines, no matter the form you choose. Those forms of project management can be broken into two distinct classifications: traditional and modern, like Agile.

When following a traditional approach, you are choosing a more conventional process with time-tested techniques. This approach can be applied to almost any field or project and has evolved over several decades. According to PMBOK, or Project Management Body of Knowledge, the traditional project management can have a standard definition to simply mean a group of methods and tools that can be geared toward an activity that has a targeted outcome, end product, or a particular service. There are a plethora of different definitions offered online, but the basics all boil back down to this standard definition provided by PMBOK.

Agile Overview

Flexibility, collaboration with the customer, and teamwork is the focus of Agile, compared to the prominence of time, scope, and cost associated with the pre-planning process for traditional project management. The Agile process dives into the changes that naturally occur and observes the effort from the group, so the customer receives results and not just an outline of a preplanned process. Project managers who have worked in the field for a long time enjoy the planning that can be adapted to various scenarios and easy changes, so they love working with Agile.

The offshoots of Agile include Kanban and Scrum. These are the two most commonly referenced by companies and professionals. Scrum has a reputation for encouraging the process of making a decision and discouraging wasting time on things that will most likely change anyway. The most important outcome for an Agile process is the satisfaction of a client. Providing the project on or ahead of schedule is one way Agile can definitely accomplish that outcome.

Traditional vs. Agile Comparison

Traditional or Other Approach	Agile
Managers control change	Teams are responsive and adaptable to changes
Process plans are the most important element	The customer's satisfaction and needs are the most essential elements
The hierarchy is strictly top-down, making the teams have to run all decisions through the manager and creating a lag in production time	Teams are self-manageable and self-sufficient; they can make quick decisions for the best of their piece as well as the overall project
Plans are created in the beginning and carried throughout the life of the project, despite changes	An evolution of the process occurs over time and speeds up as it further develops
Irrelevant metrics are ignored	The customer's delivered value is an essential measurable metric
Not inclusive or customizable	Profoundly customizable and inclusive

How Can Agile Work with Other Project Management Processes?

Several project managers have asked this question; the answer is not straightforward, however. This is because Agile can work with other processes, but it needs to be done cautiously and on different projects. Having two project management groups approach the same task in their own unique ways is not effective for many reasons, including financial and interpersonal. People working against one another like that will result in animosity rather than customer value. In addition, implementing two strategies together, such as Agile and Waterfall, could result in one canceling the other out or realizing that it is not the most effective approach. Still, it is possible.

Despite the above-mentioned suggestions for combining Agile with another process, it is also fair to explore the ideas of those opposed to the concept. The primary reason people do not believe Agile could work with another method is because of the differences between the two. In addition, the combination can cause confusion in your company and derail the progress of the project.

The Reasons Agile is Favored

There are several reasons that project managers prefer Agile to other forms of project management. Some of those reasons include the distinct sections, the internal organizational structure, and the engagement of the customer.

Divisible Sections

"Iterations" is the term assigned to the various sections a project is divided into. After one iteration is completed, it is then immediately sent to the customer. As each is sent to the customer, they can see if the project will be successful or can adjust as needed along the way. This method also allows you the freedom not to preplan the entire project.

Internal Organizational Structure

Management runs parallel to the project's iterations. Groups are managed to complete a piece of the overall project instead of having one dominant supervisor who oversees all the employees. Often in an Agile company, there can be several groups working on a specific project. Each one of the groups has an internal manager who is not guided by external pressure. Interactions between the teams only occur to discuss the project and link processes if one team lacks the ability to complete a task internally.

Most Agile projects have three components:

1. Owner - This person is the expert for the overall project and the central point of contact and review for all the teams.

2. Scrum Master - The Agile process is overseen by this role. They check in with each iteration along the way and make sure it is completed.

3. Team - The critical component to the success of each iteration is the group of employees working on completing the tasks. There are both large and small roles within a team, but they are all significant to the process of the project.

Engagement of the Customer

Engaging your customer is the primary concern in an Agile environment. As an iteration is completed and sent to the customer, the customer is responsible for giving feedback to the owner, which the team then needs to act upon.

When you compare Agile to the more traditional systems, it is obvious Agile is superior. The comparison here highlights the features of Agile and why it is considered one of the top project management systems worldwide.

Project Management Methodologies

As I was saying before, project management can be done in a thousand different ways, and given the wide range of approaches and the hundreds of combinations you can make between them, *thousands* is not even an exaggeration.

Understanding the underlying characteristics of project management and the points that bring together most of the approaches is really important in understanding how Scrum works. More than that, it is quite important for those moments when you might find yourself in the situation of bringing two or even more project management methodologies together.

To understand how project management schools of thought can be so essentially different, you should understand that there is no "right" or "wrong" approach. Some may work in some situations, while others might work in other situations, industries, and types of teams. And that is perfectly normal.

You simply cannot say about a project management methodology that it is the "best" or the "worst" in any way; they are different in nature, and they can work in different contexts to a greater or lesser extent. Even if you are the proponent of a given project management method, keeping your eyes and your mind open to other types of project management will keep you on your toes and capable of implementing the necessary adjustments to your chosen methodology when this is needed.

So, for the purpose of helping you understand the wider realm of project management theory, here are some of the most popular methodologies out there:

1. Agile. This is one of the most commonly used project management methods today, particularly in software development industries and generally technical environments.

Agile works where the project has to be iterative and incremental (or at least up to some extent). It is a project management method that relies on collaborative effort and self-reliance/organization more than anything else.

If you had to put Agile on the opposite spectrum of another project management method, that would be Waterfall.

2. Scrum. This is the main topic of the book at hand. Scrum is a project management method derived from the original Agile, which brings improvement to it by enhancing its main philosophy with

concepts like the Daily Scrum, for example.

Same as any other Agile project management method, Scrum only works in teams that can be self-reliant and disciplined. Without these two qualities of a team as a group, Scrum might not be the best solution.

Furthermore, Scrum is more suitable in cases when there is a significant degree of uncertainty and things can easily slip out of hand. Because it works in incremental steps, Scrum will make it easier to fix issues and add new items to the backlog.

3. Waterfall. Of all the project management methods out there, Waterfall is the most common and is frequently the most unrealistic one as well. In its very simplest form, Waterfall does not take into account a series of variables that might affect the good course of the project.

On the other hand, however, Waterfall is simple to understand, making it a gateway methodology for many junior project managers and helping them understand the very basics of project management.

Waterfall is, to date, one of the most popularly used project management methods in the world, even in some of the more giant corporations. For environments like that, it only makes sense to manage everything at the highest level and not split a requirement into multiple tasks, as you would from a Scrum project manager point of view.

However, even Waterfall and Scrum can be reconciled and brought together as a symbiotic system that will help you better manage the deliverables of a project.

4. Six Sigma. This is one of the most highly regarded project management methods out there. Widespread across various industries but predominantly used in the automotive one, Six Sigma is complex, intricate, and simple at the same time.

As a general rule of thumb, Six Sigma is usually seen as a problem-solving methodology, rather than a project management methodology per se. However, due to its nature and the structured way in which it approaches matters, Six Sigma tends to be popular across corporations in particular precisely because it shows a clear inclination toward documentation and procedural implementation.

5. Kanban. Although we will not discuss Kanban extensively throughout this book, it is still important that you are aware of it and its basic principles.

Same as Six Sigma, Kanban is a Lean project management methodology, and also the same as Six Sigma, it is one of the officially accepted approaches that comes under the "methodology" category as well. This status is somewhat debated in the other examples given here; however, for the purpose of this book's explanation, we will refer to Scrum as a methodology. The reason I have chosen to do this is because it does provide a system of practices and techniques that can be applied in project management.

Going back to Kanban, it can be said that it is incredibly similar to Scrum. Same as Scrum, Kanban is suitable for smaller teams who need to be Agile and easily adaptable, which is also why it makes all the sense in the world that these methods are used in software project management.

The main difference between Kanban and Scrum is, aside from the terminology used within the two systems, the fact that Kanban is even more relaxed than Scrum. While both of these project management methodologies rely on the existence of a backlog, Scrum also adds specificities about the time frame in which a project or a chunk of a project should be finished in.

6. Lean. This project management approach is frequently used in manufacturing, where quality becomes more than an issue

related to satisfying the client and more of an issue that has the potential to endanger lives.

The reason Lean project management fits into this industry so well is that it focuses a lot on removing waste and delivering a perfect product in the end. It has five associated core principles. They include value (provision of value to the intended customer or user), value stream (how value is created at the different levels of the project), flow (the cadence and the rhythm of a project's work), pull (reducing the waste), and perfection (delivering a fully functional product at the end of the project).

Six Sigma is frequently connected to the world of Lean project management as a sub-branch of it. However, their approaches are slightly different, and it is worth studying both of them should you decide to settle on any.

Over the course of this book, we will discuss how the first four of these project management methods are connected through the lens of Scrum, how they can be reconciled when different teams, on different project management methodologies work, and how Scrum can offer value to most of them when implemented as a secondary line of thought.

Principles of Agile

Agile manifesto and Associated Values

There are four key values ("What is Agile Project Management? Origins and Practices") associated with the manifesto and 12 important principles which support it. Each of the Agile methodologies is based on these principles and values.

Individuals and Participations Over Tools and Processes

It places a greater emphasis on people than the tools and processes. This is because people are the ones who respond to the needs of a business and propel its development. If the means or process spearhead development, chances are that the team will not actively participate in the changes and this has a chance to not satisfy the customer.

Working software over a detailed documentation

Traditionally, a lot of time was spent on creating a document to be used in product development and delivery. Technical requirements, specifications, test plans, documentation, and approvals were required. This extensive list caused delays in the development of software. Agile does not eliminate documentation but it provides a much better way to help the developer know what to do. Agile documents are created as user stories that are enough to help in software development. The Agile Manifesto has respect for the documentation but also gives much more respect to working software.

The partnership of customer over contract negotiation

Negotiation refers to the point when a customer and product manager sit down to come up with the project details. In a software model such as the Waterfall model, customers discuss in detail the requirements of a product in the early stages. In this case, the customer acts as a participant in the development.

However, they don't take part in product creation. The Agile Manifesto provides a platform for a customer to collaborate in the whole process of product development. Therefore, it is easy for the team to meet the needs of the customer. The Agile methods may involve the customer during different periods of the demos, but still, it can involve the end-user in the daily development. This ensures that all the requirements are achieved.

Response to change over a subsequent plan

The traditional software development methodology considers changes in software as an extra expense. As a result, it does not embrace changes. The goal is to create a comprehensive plan that has a collection of features. In this plan, all the features are marked with the highest priority. Also, there is an extensive level of dependency to help a team work on a puzzle. However, with Agile methodology, because of a short iteration, it is possible to transform priorities from one iteration to another. Additionally, new features are integrated into the next iteration.

And so, Agile provides a positive response to change. A famous example is the Method Tailoring technique. This method involves human beings determining the development approach of a system through different changes. Agile allows a team to change the process and ensure that it mirrors the needs of the user.

The 12 Agile Manifesto Principles

These principles describe a culture where change is accepted, and the customer is the center of focus. These 12 principles include:

1. Satisfying the customer through frequent software delivery. This means that customers should feel happy when they see the progress of their projects instead of waiting for the time of release.

2. Withstand changes to requirements in the entire process of development.

3. Constant delivery of software that is working.

4. A partnership between developers and business owners in the whole project.

5. Provision of trust, support, and motivation for all the people involved.

6. Provide face-to-face interactions.

7. Working software is the basis of measurement of the progress attained.

8. Agile processes to promote subsequent speed in the development.

9. Focus on the technical specs and design to improve agility.

10. Deliver simplicity. Create products in the right way to ensure everything runs well.

11. Self-organizing groups should promote better architectures, designs, and requirements.

12. A follow-up meeting to ensure that the right product is created.

The purpose of Agile is to make sure both development and business needs are on par. Agile projects are customer-friendly and motivate the customer to participate in the development. Therefore, Agile has turned out to be the game-changer in software development.

The unfortunate side effect of the Agile method is that there is no magic process or prescription to help you find a solution to your problem. While you cannot pick up an Agile book and find a plan that you can plug and play, you can find tips on how to make your Agile projects more successful. Below are the three of the premium principles you can implement to help your labors flourish.

Make Your Loop for Feedback Short

While many people identify the importance of an Agile project, they struggle to define its significance. Simply put, the shorter time between working and getting customer input on the product is a founding purpose of it all. The nightmare of hiding away for long periods of time to create an entire project only to show it to your customer who reacts negatively to the outcome can be entirely avoided with an Agile approach. Daily or at least after each iteration, the customer is involved in the process and provides feedback. This feedback is included in the next iteration, as expected. In addition, a working product can be given to the customer after a sprint or cycle for development. This delivery gives your team the opportunity for immensely valuable reviews for future changes. When you incorporate the feedback into the next workable delivery, your customer can appreciate the value of the product and your company to them. Now you are no longer checking off boxes on a plan that was established before the challenges of the project were fully realized.

Another component that is used in an Agile project is to create a test for the task you are working on to determine its practical application in the overall project. This is called TDD, or Test-Driven Development, in a software Agile environment. Coders write in a test for their piece of the project to test its overall usability before saying it is complete. If it passes the test, it is done. If not, the coder has the opportunity to find the problem and fix it before it affects other parts of the project. This process motivates team members to find the easiest and fastest method to the solution. There is no need to connect parts of the project or task unnecessarily. This concept encourages simplicity. In a coding environment, this simpler code also makes it easier for future changes and adaptations. While this feedback is not necessarily coming from the client, it is another method for shortening the cycle for feedback. While you may hear this concept referred to as another name, like Behavioral-Driven Development, or BDD, or Acceptance

Test-Drive Development, or ATDD, there are differences between the approaches despite many similarities.

Agile Works from the Inside

Internally-focused products also need to be continuously improved. This means you also need to be aware of how you can keep your internal environment competitive to offer the best to your customers. You also need to be constantly improving. When you are offering a leading company that delivers value to customers, you will find intense competition for your open positions. Think of innovative companies, inside and out, like Microsoft, Netflix, Facebook, and Google. People compete to work with them because they do not only provide value to their customers but a valuable place to work. In addition, these kinds of companies bring their development and operations teams together for the best results. Developers are making the products, making sprints, and talking about Scrum. Operators are administrators and experts who manage and deploy the products. In a more traditional environment, development creates and then passes to the operations side to deploy. They would then manage the operations of the product to ensure it functions properly. The new challenge is to integrate the two together to become more Agile.

To develop this integration, it is crucial to remove the barrier between the two departments. The two begin working together to get help on both designing and automating. This cross-functional collaboration internally is vital to the success of an Agile company. It helps each role receive valuable internal feedback to perform better and provide more value. It is no longer a pass-off but rather a team sport.

The value of the business is the focus

Ideally, you have a goal that you are measuring your progress against, so you can have a shorter feedback loop. This means every iteration or sprint results in a workable product that operates simultaneously with other products. But the primary purpose does not rely on a singular function. The primary purpose is the value that is provided to the business, especially your customer's business. Your goal is to offer them a solution to deeply employ their customers or achieve more resourcefully.

A traditional project management process has a common problem: The conception of the end product is formed at the beginning, prior to any feedback or testing of an approach's success to a problem. During this process, the customer works with you to create a laundry list of needs, and then you develop what you think will respond to those needs. This type of process means you do not interact with the customer often, but the true challenge is the dependence on the list of requirements set at the beginning rather than providing real value to the customer. Blaming the failure of the project on the list provided at the beginning is ineffective. A product will only work if it fulfills the current needs of the customer and the ultimate user in the end.

Making your feedback cycle shorter, ensuring Agile is working from the inside out, and focusing on the value of the business and product are the three primary principles of an Agile project and company. They drive most of the successful businesses in your industry and set them above the more mediocre competition. If you focus on these three primary principles, you will almost surely improve your processes and company success.

Reasons to be Agile

The beauty and the pain of project management are that it looks idyllic on paper with its "practical" applications and defined practices, but the application begins to reveal the pain of implementation. If you do not spend the time learning Agile, or any project management for that matter, and try to implement practices too quickly, you will find things to be ineffective and unbalanced. Your project will suffer from unequal risk, quality, cost, time, and scope. You and your company's culture need to be structured and prepared before taking this method on. This is why you will find those who praise Agile and those who vehemently oppose it.

To make Agile work for you and your company, you need to approach it as a tool that will assist you in running your organization; it is not your firm that is supposed to be run by Agile. Instead, it is important you discover how you can implement this Agile tool into your company's structure and values system to ensure that it complements the overarching mission of your company.

Adapting to Agile

1. Philosophize on the concept until the process engineers are not able to objectively develop the project.

2. Shift focus from the end goal to the process each time so that it becomes a habit.

Of course, there are more approaches within these two extreme examples, the reasons you should consider Agile for your company, and the methods you can take to adopt it successfully.

The History of Agile

Since it became mainstream, Agile has passed through its own waves of application and adaptation. In the beginning, it gained notoriety for its ability to help a software company get its product to market faster than using a traditional project management approach. This was termed "MVP" or "Minimum Viable Product." Now small or medium-sized companies had an implemented model to help them get more results for less time, money, etc. When these little businesses showed success with this model, larger organizations wanted to jump on board. They saw the benefit of better customer interaction and products getting to market faster.

As companies tweaked and adapted the early Agile to their businesses, another phase of Agile was created. This phase involved the businesses that did not adopt the previous methods but wanted to capitalize on the benefits. The reason this was a distinct wave in the development of Agile is that these late adopters had uncertain motivations. They also were more invested in the outcomes, as with traditional project management, than the process and customer engagement.

Each organization encounters distinctive challenges and usual problems that drive them to adopt Agile. When you can define your problem, you have the starting point for Agile. Now you can figure out how Agile will address your issue and decide the KPI's, or Key Performance Indicators, founded on these motives. While Agile may not be for every organization, there has yet to be any area discovered where it cannot be applied successfully. The best advice for adoption is to make sure the core values of Agile align well with your philosophy as a business. It is not sensible to try forcing the two to fit together.

Reasons for Adopting Agile

The best reason to adopt Agile in your company is because of its proven success in a variety of fields and projects. The process is constantly changing and quickly evolving thanks to its flexible and self-improving qualities. Other reasons to adopt Agile include: processes, self-regulation, acceptance of change, fast turnaround, customer engagement, and motivated team environment.

Process for Excellence

The path to excellence lies with consistent actions no matter what business you run. This why a business succeeds or fails; your actions are not individually spontaneous; they are practiced over and over. This means the processes you set up to complete your actions must be "right." Therefore, adopting an Agile process can dramatically help your success because it focuses on continually improving your actions to deliver the highest value to your customers. In addition, it is abstract enough to allow for customization as required. Using the processes already in place in other companies or for other projects can be adapted to suit your company's needs. Then you can logically assess how it works for you.

Self-regulation

If you are not careful, when you establish an Agile environment, success can lead to a shift in priority. Your team members will move from task-focused to role-focused. Because of the process used before, they do not want to stray from the structure of the company but rather stick with the flow. Without realizing it, it is possible to fall into a rigid bureaucracy. This type of environment removes the opportunity for taking risks, solving errors, or experimenting. This is why emphasizing the self-regulation inherent to successful Agile processes is important. This focus encourages balancing flexibility and discipline. It is not bureaucratic; it is democratic. Having a strong, self-regulated Agile process gives your team the opportunity to stay focused on the project and stay productive, instead of just completing steps to a process.

Accepting of Change

The creep that occurs in a project's scope or changes that are inherent to all tasks means it is important to accept and plan for change. The problem is that you cannot know what the changes will be until it is impossible to avoid them. Until that point, tasks are created to resist change. When it is impossible to escape, then procedures are implemented. This is not how an Agile environment approaches change and creeping scope. Instead, change is at the forefront of the process. Change is an evolution, not a limitation. This means that as changes or issues come up, they should be responded to instead of avoided. Solutions do not come prepackaged, so your teams must try out a few options until one sticks.

Fast Turnaround

Projects can be vigorous and unpredictable. As a new concept hits the market, old ones are falling away just as fast. This means it cannot take a long time for you to develop something "perfect" before you get it to the customer. In a fast-paced world, a traditional project management approach can just simply take too long. Following the "old way" means you eventually have to choose between compromising on the customer's needs or your process. Becoming Agile allows you to get a valuable product to market while still meeting the needs of the customer.

Customer Engagement

One of the major challenges in a traditional project management system is that you do not know if you met your customer's needs until you deliver the final project. This is because only the customer can tell you how they feel about the result. This separation creates an extreme problem. There have been several proposed solutions to handle this, but constant customer engagement throughout the process stands out as the best solution. This involves the customer in troubleshooting problems and addressing changes together with your teams, so they know the final solution they will receive. Creating this expectation at the beginning of the relationship allows you to emphasize the value you place on your customer more than a process.

Motivated Team Environment

Traditional project management spends a significant amount of time on planning and charting. While planning is still important, it is redirected to another place. Stakeholders used to determine roles that the project manager would assign to team members and then determine the timeline. The moment the plan was revealed to the team and the roles were assigned, it was strictly adhered to. Instead of providing guidance and accountability to the project, the method turned into a crutch that allowed the team to blame the failure or success of the project on the plan. This was because the accountability of the project was placed on the project manager, not on those carrying out the tasks. Using the Agile method, the team can take ownership of the project. When the team felt that their effort was a direct benefit or hindrance to the overall project, they felt accountable and motivated to put their best work forward. The teams work together, not as individual "worker bees." Setting up an opportunity for teams to work together cross-functionally is another benefit to this, and it makes individual teams rise to the challenge for others as well. If a team member is new, limited, or unskilled, they can still contribute to the project and group and feel important.

The final reason to adopt Agile is simple: It makes you think smarter about your company, projects, customers, and employees. Chances are, if you have tried project management or are thinking about it, one of the best reasons to adopt Agile immediately. But if that's not enough, consider the information outlined above: a new approach to your processes, self-regulation, acceptance of change, fast turnaround, customer engagement, and motivated team environment. One or all should be enough to make you ready to try an Agile approach on your next project.

Scope and Responsibilities of the Team

Creating a thriving team is one of the most important indicators for success when you migrate to an Agile environment. As a matter of fact, the Agile migration will not be successful without collaborative teams that work together efficiently and effectively together. In order to establish your Agile roles, you need to do more than just define them and plug in your team members. Instead, you must develop each role with the explicit intention of project finality, not just the preparation for the project.

This means you need to change your mindset. No longer are you ruled by the questions, "What is needed to complete the project, and whom do I have who can work on it?" These two questions can fill a defined role, but the people you have "available" may not be the best for the team or project's needs. Instead, you need to build a team that is diverse and balanced. The members should be both in possession of the skill to accomplish the tasks but also the interpersonal strengths to get it done as a collaborative team. They need to be dependable, flexible, willing, and creative. The combination of technical skill and these personality traits makes for a dynamic and successful team. And the final component of a successful team is the support you provide to them and the support they provide to one another. This goes beyond merely training them how to *be* Agile, but encouraging and supporting them as they adjust to the process is paramount.

Approaching the assignment of roles also depends on the size of the team you are working with. For example, a large environment offers more people to choose from, but more complications from previous roles. A small environment offers a speedier alteration to roles, but less to pull from. To help you define roles for your organization, the following chapter has been separated into small and large teams. Small is considered a team with fewer than 15 people and large is a team with more than 50. Teams that fall in between these numbers should read about both suggestions and come up with a solution they think will work best for their unique situation.

Small Teams

Each methodology gives their roles slightly different names; however, many of the descriptions will align with the roles listed below. At times, you will find alternative titles listed in the description to help you find the best role for your method. It is important to remember that a role is not a position in your company. A person can have multiple roles, and those roles can change occasionally or frequently depending on your company and the projects. In addition, it is possible to have more than one person assigned to a role, or no one at all. Below are the most common small-team Agile roles:

Team Leader

Also known as "Scrum Master," "Team Coach," or "Project Lead." The person in this role oversees the teams and gathers the resources necessary for the team's success. They also protect the team from outside threats. This role is more administrative, requiring more inter-personal management skills rather than technical. It is considered better to leave these technical components to the teams to work on, anyway.

Team Members

Also known as "Developer" or "Programmer." These people create and deliver the project pieces. During this process, these people model, program, test, and deliver features.

Product Owner

Also known as "On-site Customer," "Active Stakeholder," or "Stakeholder." It is a reserved role for a single person dedicated on the team to review the backlog and determine the priorities. They are responsible for making sure that decisions are speedy and also offer information quickly.

Stakeholder

Also known as "Direct User," "Indirect User," "User Manager," "Senior Manager," "Operations Manager," etc. This role is specifically for the individual paying for the completion of the project, supports the team administratively, audits the work, or generally manages the personnel. Anyone affected by the project is considered the project's stakeholders.

Technical Experts

These people are responsible for stepping in to help a team complete a task but are not a consistent member of the task force. For example, a build master may need to be called upon to write a script, or a DBA needs to be used to design and test a system. They provide a certain skill set when needed or help with a problem, and then they back out of the iteration.

Domain Experts

These people are also temporary members of the team that collaborate with the members. The people who are assigned this role are experts in a particular area, such as an expert in taxes who comes in to teach about the requirements needs from a legal perspective or an executive from a sponsor who shares the project's vision with the team.

Independent Tester

This is more than one person, generally. This group of people is not involved in the day-to-day production of the feature, but instead come in when the product is ready to be tested. They can work alongside the team, but their intention is to validate the work of the team. Many companies utilize this role when they have adequate staffing, but it is not required for your success. If you are unable to maintain an independent test team all the time, consider only assigning this role for the more detailed or large-scale projects.

Large Teams

After totaling over 20 people in a team, it is time to reconsider your roles assigned. Technically, a team is not "large" until it is over 50, but the dynamic shift between 19 and 20 is significant enough to warrant a new look. Now you may have enough to divide up and conquer more even faster! Now you can have two small teams instead of one of a larger size. Ideally, these small teams can work independently to complete the Agile task, often part of a larger project. This idea is commonly referred to as "Conway's Law" in reference to Melvin Conway, the man who outlined this concept toward the end of the 1960s. New roles for larger teams include:

Architecture Owner

This role facilitates the decisions of the architecture for the smaller teams and works closely with the overall architect owner, who manages the total direction of the architecture for the project. They lead the team to envision the architecture because they helped develop the total vision in the beginning. Do not confuse this role with the traditional architect because they are not creating the direction of the entire project, but rather, they are assisting with the formation and development of the plan.

Integrator

When there are two or more sub-teams or small teams working for a larger project, at some point the sub-teams need to integrate their work. At times, there will be a large team working on a complicated task, while there are a few small teams working on smaller iterations. Integrators gather the pieces from the various teams and begin to put them together into the final project. This role functions well with the independent testers it has been assigned because as the integrator combines the pieces, it is important to test the combination to make sure it functions properly.

The Absence of Traditional Roles

It may sound like most of the "old" roles have been eliminated, but after careful consideration, it is evident that these "new" Agile roles combine what used to be the Project Manager or Business Analyst, with roles like Team Coach or Team Members. This means the functions of those roles still occur, but in a different capacity than before.

The Absence of Enterprise Roles

The primary purpose of this section has been to identify the team and organizational roles on an Agile team, not on the role of enterprise-level support, like the Enterprise Admin or Portfolio Manager. To be able to scale your Agile methods better, you need to also create enterprise-level Agile positions. While they may not hold a role on the teams, they can and should still embrace the Agile mindset for the betterment and success of the teams and company in general.

Chapter 6:
Kanban System: A Start-Up's Process Management

The Kanban system is a system used to schedule just-in-time manufacturing and lean manufacturing. In Japanese, Kanban literally means billboard or signboard. A Toyota industrial engineer, Taiichi Ohno, came up with Kanban to increase their manufacturing efficiency ("Everything You Need to Know About Kanban Cards," 2016). The name was derived from the cards the factory used to track production. For those that work in the automotive industry, Kanban is known to all as the "Toyota nameplate system." This is the reason why other automobile manufacturers don't want to use the term Kanban.

Kanban immediately became useful in helping support a production system and promoting further improvement. The system is used to find problem areas by measuring lead times and the cycle of the process and its steps. The most significant benefit of Kanban is that it creates upper limits to work in process inventory to prevent overcapacity.

One of the main goals of the system is preventing excess inventory buildup within the production areas. Limits are placed on items stored at supply points. Once inefficiencies are identified, the limits are reduced and then eventually removed. When limits are exceeded, the identified inefficiency will be taken care of.

History

The Kanban system originated from an empty box, which was just a simple replenishment signaling system. The UK Spitfire factories first developed this during the war, and they referred to it as the "two-bin system." Then, in the late '40s, Toyota began to search in supermarkets looking for shelf-stocking methods to use on their factory floor.

When it comes to grocery stores, customers will typically get what they need at the needed time. Furthermore, customers only take what they need, knowing there will surely be a future supply. This is why grocery stores only stock things expected to sell at a particular time. Noticing this, Toyota started to compare a process to a customer from previous processes, as well as the previous processes to a store.

Kanban is used to align the levels of inventory with consumption. There will be a signal indicating that a specific material was already consumed, and the supplier now needs to deliver a new shipment. The replenishment cycle will track these signals, which will bring visibility to the buyer, supplier, and consumer.

The demand rate is what Kanban uses to control the production rate. The demand is passed from the very last buyer up to the store processes. In 1953, Toyota applied this new idea in their machine shop.

Toyota Operations

A demand forecasting needed a push, which is why production scheduling was a success. On the contrary, Kanban approaches by pulling from the demand before ordering the product. Production and re-supply will be figured out based on customer orders.

When the supply time becomes too long, and the demand is still uncertain, the best thing to do is to respond quickly when a demand is noticed. The Kanban system excels this way. The Kanban system acts as a demand signal which will soon make its way to the supply chain. This will ensure better management and a smaller amount of the intermediate stock in the supply chain. When the response to supply is slower than the demand fluctuations, which causes a possible lost sale, the building of stock may be appropriately considered. Kanban is then added to the system to reach the required stock.

Taiichi Ohno explains that for a Kanban system to be effective, it has to follow strict rules. Toyota came up with a list of six rules. They have to constantly monitor those rules, which will ensure that their Kanban system does exactly what it needs to.

The six rules that Toyota formulated for their Kanban application are:

1. All processes will provide a request to its supplier as the supplies are consumed.

2. All processes are produced based upon the sequence and quantity of incoming requests.

3. Without a request, nothing will be made or delivered.

4. The request is always attached to the item.

5. Processes have to ensure that they only deliver defect-free items.

6. Pending requests should be limited to make sure that the processes are sensitive and determine the inefficiencies.

Cards

The Kanban cards help in signaling the movement of the materials as well as in switching materials from the outside supplier to the main production facility, making it an essential part of the Kanban system. This card is like a message showing the depletion of parts, products, or inventory. When Kanban receives the message, it will trigger the replenishment of that particular part, product, or inventory. The consumption will trigger the demand for additional production, while the card will prompt the demand for products. In simpler terms, the Kanban cards produce a system driven by demands.

In terms of lean production proponents, they have always believed that demand-driven systems will lead to lower inventory levels and quicker turnarounds. This ends up helping companies be more competitive by implementing these types of systems.

Systems that use Kanban signals have become increasingly popular over the last couple of years. This new trend has reduced the usage of Kanban cards. However, it is still commonly used in modern production facilities. Kanban uses email notification in signaling demand to the suppliers. It can also be used in various kinds of software systems. A "Kanban trigger" will be activated when a specific part has hit a lower amount than the number that was indicated on the card. It will demand a purchase order with set quantities to the suppliers. The supplier then needs to fulfill the request within the specified time.

While Kanban cards have stuck to the primary principles of Kanban, it still needs extra materials. There's a need for more parts if an empty bin contains a red card.

Three-Bin System

A good example of the Kanban system is the "three-bin system." This is used in the absence of in-house manufacturing of supplied parts. Their initial demand point is the bin found on the floor of the factory. The inventory control point is the bin located in the factory store. Finally, the supplier has the last bin. The classic Kanban cards are removable cards found in each bin, which contain the details and other important facts about the product.

Since the parts inside the bin positioned on the factory floor are used for manufacturing and are often empty, the bin, along with its Kanban card, is sent to the store. The store will replace the emptied bin with a full one that also has its own Kanban card. The empty bin will then be sent out to the supplier from the factory store.

The supplier will eventually give its product bin with the card back to the factory store. The empty bin is now at the supplier. This is the last step in the process, meaning it will never run out of the product. It can also be considered a closed-loop process. This is because it only gives the exact amount of the product needed in a single bin without worrying about oversupply. The spare bin will allow for any uncertainties in supply, transport, and use. The best system will compute enough Kanban cards in correlation to each product. The heijunka box, a colored-board system, is commonly used in many major factories.

Electronic

Several manufacturers have started to use an electronic Kanban system, which will help to reduce the common problems like lost cards and manual entry errors. Electronic systems can be used in enterprise resource planning systems, which will enable real-time demand signals throughout the supply chain as well as improve visibility. Tracking the supplier leads and the replenishment times from the date taken from the electronic system can improve the levels of the inventory.

Functioning as a signaling system, the Electronic Kanban uses a combination of technology in triggering the movement of the materials, both in the manufacturing and production. The use of technology such as barcodes differentiates this kind of Kanban from the original, which still uses cards and email messages.

Inventory is typically marked with barcodes, which a worker uses at the process' various stages to identify usage. Messages are sent out through the scans to the external and internal stores to ensure that the products are restocked. The messages are routed to the suppliers through the internet. The inventory can also be viewed in real-time.

Organizations like Bombardier Aerospace and Ford Motor Company have improved their processes using electronic Kanban systems. You can see widespread use of these systems from bolt-on modules or single solutions to ERP systems.

Systems

Adjacent upstream and downstream workstations talk to each other within the Kanban system through their cards, where all bins have an associated Kanban. An essential part of this is Economic Order Quantity. The more popular types of Kanban systems are:

- Transportation Kanban – This authorizes the transport of a full bin to a workstation downstream. This is also found in the bins that are connected to the transportation to move throughout the loop again.

- Production Kanban – Once received, this Kanban authorizes a station to make a definite number of products. The containers associated with it carry this Kanban.

Utilizing Kanban

There are three primary parts to Kanban, no matter if you look at examples from a Toyota factory in the 1950s or on a Lean practitioners Kanban app. The three elements are the board, list, and card. Essentially, the board contains a list, which creates the workflows from the various cards. Each is defined below:

1. Board: This is what houses the workflow (Miller, 2019). In other project management processes, this is referred to as a "workspace" or "project."

2. List: Also called a "lane," this has a series of aligned cards, usually related to the same part of the production line, and is the title of a column on a board. In other

project management systems, it is called the to-do or task list.

3. Card: A card is found under a list title on a board. This is a product that should be created or a given task to be achieved. These are actionable items. In other systems, these are called "tasks" or "to-dos."

A Kanban board is as versatile as an Excel spreadsheet; its applications are endless. For example, if you are about to launch a new product, you can have two Kanban boards, one for marketing and one for development. Marketing would create a board with lists titled "Internal Promotion," "Press Pitches," and "Marketing Ideas." Development would create lists such as "To-do," "Doing," and "Done." Each department would then create task cards to move from one column to the other as they bring up and complete each task.

While this example above only offers two ideas in a non-manufacturing setting, there are many more applications to explore. But no matter how you want to implement a board, you need to master the basics of moving from just having a list and a bunch of cards to developing an efficient and orderly workflow.

10 Primary Features of a Kanban Board

The features presented in this section all function primarily the same, no matter how you implement it. Some features only apply to an electronic version of the Kanban system, such as a Kanban app, while others refer to both a physical Kanban board and an electronic app. In addition, the names and titles may depend on the practitioner or app you use, but again, the functionalities are always similar.

Boards and Lists are Filled with Moving Cards

Being able to move cards around quickly is critical to effectively utilizing Kanban boards. It is the most utilized feature in a Kanban model. In fact, the existing cards you have on the board will move more than the new ones you create. In an app, you can click on the card, hold down the button on your mouse, and move your cursor to a new location. This action allows you to move your card from one list to another or to change the location of the card on the existing list. Because this is a feature you will often utilize if you are using an app, find out what process works with the app you have chosen and become familiar with the layout and functionality as soon as possible. For example, LeanKit offers the ability to change list locations. You can have a higher or lower list, and you will need to know how to drag a card between them. Try it out and find where and how you can move your cards. After all, you cannot break it!

Unlike in a manual or physical board situation, you can look back on the path each card has taken on your Kanban board. When you move a card on a physical board, you will either have to take pictures or mentally remember where it was to know its journey throughout the process. In an app, technology keeps track for you. In many apps, when you click on the card, it will "flip over" to reveal its backside. Here it will often show you its activity list. Much more efficient than the manual way!

People are Invited to A Kanban Board, and Assignments and Subscriptions of Individual Cards are Outlined

As with other project management systems, collaborators, clients, and teammates can be invited to the project. An invitation can be extended through the app for access to the entire board or only for an individual card. Some apps only allow you to invite app members to the board while others will allow you to invite anyone by entering their name and email into the invitation fields. After they are added to the board, they can then act on the cards. If a member is added to a single card, they can only act on that card. Typically, they can edit a card, comment on them, move or add them. In addition, they can also observe the stream of activity relevant to the board they are a part of. This allows the members to see the project process even if they are not an active part of the tasks.

To assign or share the responsibility of a task you can add a card to a member or user. This prompts the app to send notifications related to the activities for the card. If your card gets a comment, for example, you will receive a notification. If someone else is assigned that card, they will get the notification as well. When someone wants to follow the progress of a card but are not responsible for the activities, many apps provide the option to "subscribe" to it. This allows the member to monitor the activity and receive notifications but not act on the card. On the other hand, if you want to "unfollow" the activities of a card, you can unsubscribe from it. This is a good practice when you want to keep your inbox free from unnecessary notifications.

On the Backs of Cards, Include Notes or Communicate in Related Discussions

In a physical setting, your comments are confined to the size of a post-it. You can only communicate until the post-it is full. Then you run out of space, and the dialogue comes to a fork in the road. In a technological setting, space is boundless. This is another distinct advantage of a virtual board over a physical option. Now you can jot down everything necessary related to the card.

Typically, on the backside of the card, there are fields for card descriptions, a place to upload related files, and a discussion forum. Also, similar to tagging someone on Twitter, you can mention a person directly in the comment or description by writing, "@-(their username)." To access the back of the card, click on the card itself to flip it over or find the link that lists additional features for the card and select "back of card" or another similar phrase.

Cards Can Have Tasks or Checklists Attached

A card needs a checklist because each task is not always a simple situation. In a virtual board, the cards can contain 1 or more task lists or checklists to make the card more functional. Thinking back to the marketing example introduced at the beginning of this chapter, the marketing department had a list titled "Press Pitches." Under this list, there is a card labeled "Outreach." On this card there is a checklist containing the following to-do items:

- Create a preliminary email for the pitch

- Complete follow-up communication with additional details

- Deliver media assets

- Confirm coverage

- Publish coverage

In some apps, the front of the card illustrates the status and progress of the checklist, showing a stage of completion as each task is checked off. This way each member can easily see the progress of the card. Similar to discussions and notes, checklists can have specific member's names included by using the same format: "@-(their username)."

Limits to Work in Progress Included

For new practitioners, creating epic task lists can be exciting but overwhelming for all involved. This is why several apps provide the option to limit the number of tasks that can be created in a list and offer WIP's, or work in progress limits ("What is Kanban"). WIP's are pronounced like "whips." This restriction can be applied to one or all columns on a board, so you have a limit to the number of cards allowed on the list.

When you know the workload your team can realistically handle, you can set your limits accordingly. For example, if your marketing team can realistically produce 3 pitches per week, then set the limit for "Press Pitches" to no more than 3 cards.

Cards can be Tagged or Labeled

A "label" or "tag" allows you to clarify specific details of a card that cannot be immediately determined by its location on the list. Your administrator or app will determine if this clarification process is called "tagging" or "labeling." Both terms are synonymous at this point in the Kanban process.

For example, if a marketing idea is for an online publication and not for a print campaign, you can add a label to the card to denote that it will be published electronically. Maybe a card requires outside assistance from another department or one task is more challenging than another; both are situations where you need a clear label. Tags are created uniquely for each board you operate. Change the label's names and colors to fit the workflow for the board you are working on.

Due Dates can be Assigned to Cards

When there is not a due date on a card, it probably will not get done. Deadlines are essential to getting tasks completed. Depending on the app you are using, you can click on the clock icon on a card or find the field for the deadline on the back of the card. Typically, there is a drop-down menu that allows you to select the date the card must be finished by.

Besides setting the date, the people assigned or subscribed to the card can also get notifications when the deadline is approaching and when something is considered overdue.

View a Calendar with Cards

Another added benefit of an electronic app is that it offers a seamless calendar view related to the board. In an app, the ability to switch from the "standard" board view to a calendar view is a simple toggle of a switch. This view will show all the advancing deadlines, schedules, and delivery dates for tasks. In this view you can also edit, move and add cards. If something is overdue or cannot be completed by its original deadline, you can drag the card to a new date to reset the deadline.

Benefits of Kanban

In the early 2000s, business leaders became interested in Kanban when it was mainly used by software developers to improve workflow. Today, it has started to be used across all disciplines to help teams visualize, optimize, and manage their work.

Even science agreed on the benefits of Kanban. Visual information can be processed by the brain 60,000 times quicker than with words. Kanban kicks understanding and communication by using visual information, into high gear.

Let's look at the several benefits your team can reap from using Kanban (Radigan, 2019).

Versatility

The main point behind the Kanban system is communication with the use of visual signals. This benefits industries and job titles everywhere. Kanban can be applied anywhere. Any company can use Kanban either from the marketing department or engineering. It's easier for projects and team members to move through various functions smoothly because of Kanban's versatility. An example of it is when moving content project to graphics from editing, or a new feature to testing from integration.

Continuous Improvement

Kanban's main principle encourages people to focus more on continuous improvement. The reviewing process is a lot easier due to the project management's visual system, as well as making necessary improvements to streamline workflow, remove the waste, and reduce overhead.

Responsiveness

Within the auto industry, where Kanban got its start, it uses the process when low in inventory, creating a better method of matching demand and inventory. When used in project management, responsiveness is still a huge benefit of Kanban. With Kanban, responding to business needs in a more Agile way is much easier.

Increased Output

The team can limit the work in progress, called limiting "WIP," using the Kanban system. Doing this, the teams are encouraged to work closely with each other in removing distractions and multitasking to finish their work. The teams can get more things done because of the improvement in intense focus and collaboration. With a more focused delivery, high-priority and high-value work items are expedited while delivering value to the business. Personal WIP limits help to relieve teams from overburdening because they can focus on a finite number of work items. They only move on to the next item in the input queue when the item that they were initially committed to is completely finished.

Empowered Teams

The whole team is in control of the Kanban system, and they share responsibilities for finishing the work. Kanban helps to empower the team to make Agile decisions that move the project forward with efficiency and innovation. The typical siloed organizations that battle between product management and software delivery become more integrated into the development value stream. Kanban encourages synergy between groups and helps to break down the walls between different specializations, which results in a collaboration between functions. Work item transitions between columns on the board will offer opportunities for communication, collaboration, knowledge discovery, and involvement and engagement for all.

A Perfect Product

Projects typically make their way to the finish line with fewer reworks and errors because of the increased concentration on continuous improvement and quick-response. Quality control can now be allowed in project management in order to give more accurate results. Looking at it from a nontechnical perspective, there are lots of activities that contribute to high-quality software, like collaborative analysis and user documentation.

Even within disciplined teams, collective behavior is controlled by rules. The policies will help to solidify the professional standards that are agreed on across the board, which includes software teams, product and project managers, and stakeholders.

Business Value First

Kanban is positioned to be a decision management framework, which makes it a lot more powerful than it looks from an outsider's view. It isn't just some board hung up on the wall! It helps to promote economically-based decision-making by managing and prioritizing work based on specific economic goals. Organizations are trying to survive in fiercely competitive environments. This means that we need to execute, identify, and prioritize the most valuable work so that the business can keep afloat and ahead of the competition.

Visibility

An amazing thing about most organizations is the amount of work that happens under the parapet. One of the core practices of Kanban is to make invisible work visible! By using a Kanban board as an information center, as well as its other merits, you will have a holistic view of process inefficiencies, blockers, impediments, bottlenecks, and progress at one glance.

Information can be easily found by not only the team members but by the external observers and stakeholders. This promotes a boundaryless flow of information across the entire organization.

Reduction of Wasteful Activities

The majority of project managers will focus most on the timeline instead of the process queues. Timelines are a part of the manager's psyche, along with Gantt charts, spreadsheets, and other time-bound documents. They don't like to embrace uncertainty. With the reinforcement of WIP limits, a Kanban board turns into a pull-based system, which keeps a reliable amount of high-quality ideas that are delivered JIT (Just in Time), while getting rid of wasteful work and lower queues. Upstream activities like business cases, discovery workshops, and requirement gathering, take place on demand and when they have to, which forces the team to make timely decisions.

Sustainability

Kanban systems help to manage your work at a sustainable, smooth, and easy pace, without any uncontrollable nadirs and distressing peaks, which only cause frustration, high employee turnover, and lack of commitment. Sustainable development brings about creativity, as WIP limits help to control the pace dynamically without fear of breaking a promise down the road. This allows for innovation, addresses issues in a new way, and produces solutions with fewer issues in quality.

Conclusion

You now have the foundational knowledge needed to enter the world of being a servant leader. Being a servant leader is prioritizing serving others. It may sound ineffective, but this allows your team members or those you oversee to flourish and work as effectively as possible. Treating your employees with respect and consideration will also help you work together and serve others in the smoothest way possible.

But reading about servant leadership is not enough. The lessons that you learned in this book can only be used to greatest effect when you set time and practice all the steps.

Changing your leadership style or assuming a leadership role may seem intimidating, but only positive things can come from such an endeavor. Get out of your comfort zone and be a great servant leader.

Thank you and enjoy the journey!

References

Agile Project Management and Scrum | Planview LeanKit. (2019). *Planview*. Retrieved 23 May 2019, from https://www.planview.com/resources/articles/agile-project-management-scrum/

Agile Project Management. (n.d.). *www.tutorialspoint.com*. Retrieved 23 May 2019, from https://www.tutorialspoint.com/management_concepts/agile_project_management.htm

Casali, D. (2015). *The Six Styles of Leadership. Intense Minimalism*. Retrieved 23 May 2019, from https://intenseminimalism.com/2015/the-six-styles-of-leadership/

Cherry, K. (2019). *What Are Prominent Leadership Styles and Frameworks You Should Know? Verywell Mind*. Retrieved 23 May 2019, from https://www.verywellmind.com/leadership-styles-2795312

Entschev, B. (2018). *Effective Communication: Key to Leadership Success - AIMS International. Aimsinternational.com*. Retrieved 23 May 2019, from

https://aimsinternational.com/news/2018/11/15
/effective-communication-key-to-leadership-
success/

*Everything You Need to Know About Kanban
Cards*. (2016). *Smartsheet*. Retrieved 23 May
2019, from
https://www.smartsheet.com/everything-you-
need-know-about-kanban-cards

Grote, D. (2016). *A Step-by-Step Guide to Firing
Someone. Harvard Business Review*. Retrieved
23 May 2019, from https://hbr.org/2016/02/a-
step-by-step-guide-to-firing-someone

Hasan, S. (2017). *Top 10 Leadership Qualities
That Make Good Leaders. TaskQue*. Retrieved 23
May 2019, from
https://blog.taskque.com/characteristics-good-
leaders/

*Leadership StylesChoosing the Right Approach
for the Situation*. (2018). *Mindtools.com*.
Retrieved 23 May 2019, from
https://www.mindtools.com/pages/article/newL
DR_84.htm

Listening Styles. (2019). *Saylordotorg.github.io*.
Retrieved 23 May 2019, from
https://saylordotorg.github.io/text_stand-up-
speak-out-the-practice-and-ethics-of-public-
speaking/s07-02-listening-styles.html

Managing Workplace Conflict. (2018). *SHRM.* Retrieved 23 May 2019, from https://www.shrm.org/resourcesandtools/tools-and-samples/toolkits/pages/managingworkplaceconflict.aspx

Mayne, D. (2019) *12 Tips to Improve Your Leadership Style. The Spruce.* Retrieved 23 May 2019, from https://www.thespruce.com/leadership-etiquette-1216825

Miller, F. (2019). *What is a Kanban Board? Why and When to Use Kanban? - Productivity Land. Productivity Land.* Retrieved 23 May 2019, from https://productivityland.com/blog/what-is-kanban-board/

Radigan, D. (2019). *Kanban - A brief introduction | Atlassian.* Retrieved 23 May 2019, from https://www.atlassian.com/agile/kanban

Stoner, J. (2012). *How to Influence Without Authority | Jesse Lyn Stoner. Seapoint Center for Collaborative Leadership.* Retrieved 23 May 2019, from https://seapointcenter.com/influence-without-authority/

Tracy, B. (2018). *7 Leadership Qualities & Characteristics of Good Leaders | Brian Tracy.*

Retrieved from
https://www.briantracy.com/blog/leadership-success/the-seven-leadership-qualities-of-great-leaders-strategic-planning/

Types of Listening | SkillsYouNeed. (2019). *Skillsyouneed.com.* Retrieved 23 May 2019, from https://www.skillsyouneed.com/ips/listening-types.html

Varhol, P. (n.d.). *The complete history of agile software development. TechBeacon.* Retrieved 23 May 2019, from https://techbeacon.com/app-dev-testing/agility-beyond-history-legacy-agile-development

What is Agile Project Management? Origins and Practices. (n.d.). *Pmis-consulting.com.* Retrieved 23 May 2019, from https://www.pmis-consulting.com/articles/agile-project-management/

What is Kanban? Comprehensive Overview of the Kanban Method. (n.d.). *Digite.* Retrieved 23 May 2019, from https://www.digite.com/kanban/what-is-kanban/

What Is Leadership? (2019). *Mindtools.com.* Retrieved 23 May 2019, from https://www.mindtools.com/pages/article/newLDR_41.htm